Practical Tajweed

Through Juz

'Amma

A Gradual Course in Qur'anic Recitation

Bint 'Abd Al Hannan Al Britaaniyyah

Title: Practical Tajweed Through Juz 'Amma

Author: Bint 'Abd Al Hannan Al Britaaniyyah

First Edition, 2023

Published in the United Kingdom

ISBN: 9798390384954

Imprint: Independently published

Table of Contents

Dedicated to the pleasure of the Creator and the service of His deen. May Allah allow us to be sincere, do that which pleases Him and keep us away from His disobedience, with goodness and blessings. Ameen.

Please contact sisterskhidmah@gmail.com for any queries.

Introduction

BismiLlah, wal ḥamdu liLlah, wa SallAllahu wa sallam 'alaa Sayyidinaa Nabiyyinaa Muḥammad wa 'alaa aalihi wa Saḥbihi ajma'een.

In the name of Allah for Whom all praises are due. May He send His blessings and peace upon our beloved Master and Noble Prophet, Sayyidunaa Muḥammad, his esteemed family and noble companions.

As for what proceeds, this is a brief work directed to the beginner student of Qur'an. After much deliberation and concern for the difficulties being faced by the seekers of the Qur'an, I contemplated on how the teaching of the noble Qur'an can be facilitated for the beginners. This started with a tiny Tajweed PocketMod booklet geared towards children and extended to a two-volume series called "Access to the Qur'an". This series aimed to give students the ability to practise their pronunciation and learn the rules of Tajweed in a more logical and simpler fashion. The focus has been heavily centred around *practise* and application of rules as a pose to mere memorisation and repetition of rules.

This work is, essentially, a step further from the "Access to the Qur'an". Herein, students are taken from Surat Al Fatihah and Surat Al Naas to Surat Al Naba', whilst mildly encountering rules in the order of relevance according to the surah. As such, it may seem that the rules are scattered, however, it is upon the student to gather those notes and recall them as is needed. The main focus should always be application of the Tajweed rules and, secondarily, to memorise juz 'amma as well as possible, inshaa Allah.

I pray that this work benefits those who utilise it and that it opens the door to a lifetime of Qur'anic study and devotion. Ameen ya Rabb. Indeed, the best of mankind are those who learn the Qur'an and teach it, as our Beloved Prophet, sallAllahu 'alaihi wa sallam, indicated towards.

Compiler's Introduction

As is the habit of those special and blessed scholars who are my role models and predecessors, in this page I will briefly introduce myself. I believe that every student has the right to have confidence in their facilitator. This is an *amaanah* (trust) of knowledge.

Firstly, I have purposely obscured my name, knowing that this is not academically correct. I do this mainly out of modesty. I do not wish for many people to come to know of me unless they have a genuine need- for which reason I have provided an email address that I can be contacted at. I will be happy to substantiate what I mention here inshaa Allah. Sufficient to say is that I am from Birmingham, UK and I was born in the early 1990s.

Henceforth is an outline of my studies:

The journey in Tajweed for me began towards the beginning of 2010 after discovering online platforms to study, such as Sunnipath and Seekersguidance- studying with Ustaadhah Sumayyah (wife of Shaykh Sulayman Van Ael), progressing onto Mufti Muhammad 'Umer Esmail (D2019- may Allah have mercy on his soul and enlighten his grave, ameen) with whom I took the vast bulk of my basic Tajweed knowledge. He granted an ijazah in teaching Tajweed and in the poem of Tuhfat Al ATfaal (year 2011). With Mufti 'Umer, I also had a chance to study most of the Jazariyyah and the usool of the Shatibiyyah. Around this time, I also completed a very basic certification in Juz 'amma with Ustaadhah Sawsan Mostafa (Egypt). I had been teaching from 2010 after being compelled to do so and by His mercy have continuously done so till today. Al hamdu lillah.

As my studies in Tajweed became more serious, Allah opened my heart to knowledge and a fresh zeal to study the Islamic sciences ensued. I was guided to a local institute where I spent the next eight years studying part time, graduating in 2019 by Allah's grace. Once this phase had been completed, I returned to my long due studies in Tajweed. I studied the Jazariyyah again with Shaykh 'Uthman Khan and also the Khaaqaaniyyah. Thereafter, I found my dear teacher Ustaadhah Hind Salem (Egypt) with whom I completed a full khatmah of the Qur'an, by the riwaayah of Hafs 'an 'Aasim min Tariq Al Shatibiyyah, mostly by looking, but with three ajzaa from memory (2019). My teacher generously granted me an ijazah to teach.

In 2020, I finally received ijazah in the Jazariyyah from Ustaadhah Zahrah Ahmath. Thereafter, I also received ijaazah in the Khaaqaaniyyah with her in 2021. I am still a seeker of this blessed science and the Noble Qur'an Al Kareem. I believe in gradual study and consolidation; therefore, this journey is ongoing inshaa Allah. Outside of Tajweed and Qur'an, Al hamdu lillah, I also received the Ibn Hajr Al 'Asqalani Hadith diploma from Shaykh Muhammad Daniel (hafidhahuAllah) of Cordoba Academy in 2021. Herein I studied basic texts on the science of hadeeth. Currently, I am focusing on studying *fiqh* and working on Qur'anic memorisation.

May Allah preserve His blessings upon us and allow us to serve His deen until the very end. Ameen.

Bint 'Abd Al Hannan Al Britaaniyyah sisterskhidmah@gmail.com

Notes on the Methodology of this Book

❖ This work and course must be supervised by a proficient teacher.

❖ The teacher may expand on relevant points and clarify any subtle ambiguities students may have.

❖ One will find a table of Tajweed rules which will help a student visualise which rules are being completed as the lessons progress.

❖ The rules are mentioned as concisely as possible, yet there is still an effort to explain the theory as simply as possible.

❖ Sometimes letters are presented using the 'Arabic text and at other times the English transliteration is used. There is no particular system to the transliteration, however, there has been an effort to differentiate letters as much as possible.

❖ Examples will seldom be presented. The student is expected to annotate their portion themselves and consolidate their application by finding more examples then practising profusely.

❖ A notes section is provided if there is space under the portion presented. If the portion and/or rules are too long, the notes section is omitted.

❖ The student should have a notebook to gather theoretical knowledge and, preferably, a diary to mark their progress.

❖ The concepts are explained in English and students are not expected to know any 'Arabic terms if they do not know the language. However, the 'Arabic term for the rules are mentioned in brackets at the end of a rule- this is to accommodate those who do not understand the language and those who do. Remember, if a student wishes to progress in their journey, they will have an opportunity to study to an advanced level later on.

❖ Also in brackets, the student will find a number reference. This leads back to the Tajweed rules in the table found at the beginning of the book.

❖ It is expected that the student would have already learnt the preliminaries and exit points from the basic primer they should have completed before this book. Many more examples and visual demonstrations are found in the "Access to the Qur'an" series.

Recitation Feedback Table

Lesson	1st Reading	2nd Reading	3rd Reading	Teacher Pass
1				
2				
3				
4				
5				
6				
7				

8				
9				
10				
11				
12				
13				
14				

15				
16				
17				
18				
19				
20				
21				

22				
23				
24				
25				
26				
27				
28				

29				
30				
31				
32				
33				
34				
35				

36				
37				
38				
39				
40				
41				
42				

43				
44				
45				
46				
47				

Table of Tajweed Rules

- ❖ As you pass the rules throughout the Qur'anic passages, write a summary of each rule within a notebook based on the table below.
- ❖ In your summary write down if the rule is an inherent quality of the letter or whether it is temporary.
- ❖ If it is temporary, clearly indicate which letter is being affected, which letter/vowel affects it and why there is this effect.
- ❖ For the advanced student and the expert, one may look into various books of Tajweed and do extra research on the rules.
- ❖ The terms included are subjective and upon a teacher to explain all points.
- ❖ It is expected that the student has already learnt the preliminaries and exit points from a basic primer before this book.

		TAJWEED			
	Lesson Reference (If applicable)	*'Arabic/English Rule Name*	*Summary (Tick)*	*Examples (If Applicable) (Tick)*	*Extra Notes from the Books with References. (Tick)*
		1. PRELIMINARIES (TO BE DONE IN ADVANCE)			
1.1	N/A	Fathah / Two Fathahs			
1.2	N/A	Kasrah / Two Kasrahs			
1.3	N/A	Dhammah / Two Dhammahs			
1.4	N/A	Sukoon			
1.5	L3-	Shaddah (Plus Nasalisation of Noon & Meem)			
1.6	N/A	Long Vowels			

1.7	N/A	Joining Hamzah & Independent Hamzah			
		2. *MAKHAARIJ (TO BE DONE IN ADVANCE)*			
2.1	L1-	Letters of the Throat/ *Huroof Al Halq*			
2.2	N/A	Letters of the Lips/ *Huroof Al Shafatayn*			
2.3	N/A	Letters of the Nasal Cavity/ *Huroof Al Khaishoom*			
2.4	N/A	Letters of the Oral Cavity/ *Huroof Al Jawf*			
2.5	N/A	Letters of the Tongue (Back) /*Huroof Al Lisaan*			
2.6	N/A	Letters of the Tongue (Middle) /*Huroof Al Lisaan*			
2.7	N/A	Letters of the Tongue (Sides) /*Huroof Al Lisaan*			
2.8	N/A	Letters of the Tongue (Tip) /*Huroof Al Lisaan*			
		3. *SIFAAT 'AARIDHAH (TEMPORARY QUALITIES)*			
3.1	L1- L5-	Laam in the name Allah/ *Laam Al Jalaalah*			
3.2	L3- L4-	Vowelled Raa/ *Raa Mutaharrikah*			
3.3	L9- L14- L15-	Non-Vowelled Raa/ *Raa Saakinah*			

3.4	L29- L30-	Non-Vowelled Raa/ *Raa Saakinah (Exceptions)*			
3.5	L11-	Meem Saakinah- Merging/ *Idghaam*			
3.6	L12-	Meem Saakinah- Labial Hiding/ *Ikhfaa Shafawi*			
3.7	L21-	Meem Saakinah- Clarity/ *Idh'haar Shafawi*			
3.8	L4-	Noon Saakinah- Clarity/ *Idh'haar*			
3.9	L5- L6-	Noon Saakinah- Merging/ *Idghaam*			
3.10	L10-	Noon Saakinah- Hiding/ *Ikhfaa*			
3.11	L13-	Noon Saakinah- Changing/ *Iqlaab*			
3.12	L24-	Mudood-Natural Prolongation/ *Madd Asli*			
3.13	L8-	Mudood- Secondary Prolongation due to Hamza/ *Madd Muttasil/Madd Munfasil*			
3.14	L24-	Mudood- Secondary Prolongation due to Sukoon or Shaddah/ *Madd Laazim*			

3.15	L17- L22-	Mudood- Extra Secondary Prolongations/ *Madd 'Aaridh* (Temporary Stretch)/ *Madd Silah* (Joining Stretch)			
3.16	L7- L24-	Mudood- Extra Secondary Prolongations/ *Madd 'Iwadh* (Substitutive Stretch)/ *Madd Badal* (Exchanged Stretch)/ Madd Leen (Soft Stretch)			
3.17	L31-	Idghaam- Minor Merging *Idghaam Sagheer*			
3.18	L32-	Idghaam- Major Merging *Idghaam Kabeer*			
3.19	L33-	Idghaam- Merging Between Two Equivalent Letters *Idghaam Mutamaathilayn*			
3.20	L34-	Idghaam- Merging Between Two Letters of the Same Genus *Idghaam Mutajaanisayn*			
3.21	L35-	Idghaam- Merging Between Two Close Letters *Idghaam Mutaqaaribayn*			

3.22	L36-	Idh'haar- Clarity Between Two Distant Letters **Idh'haar Mutabaa'idayn**			
3.23	L38-	Idghaam- Complete Merging **Idghaam Kaamil**			
3.24	L39-	Idghaam- Incomplete Merging **Idghaam Naaqis**			
		4. *SIFAAT LAAZIMAH (PERMANENT QUALITIES)*			
4.1	L6- L23- L25-	With Opposites- Voiceless Letters/ Voiced Letters/ **Hams & Jahr**			
4.2	L2- L6- L18- L20- L23- L25-	With Opposites- Sound Continuous Letters/ Sound Stopping Letters/ **Rikhawah & Shiddah (with Tawassut)**			
4.3	L26-	With Opposites- Depressed Letters/ Elevated Letters/ **Istifaal & Isti'laa'**			
4.4	L26-	With Opposites- Non-Adhered Letters/ Adhered Letters/ **Infitaah & ITbaaq**			

4.5	L26-	With Opposites- Fluent Letters/ Hindered Letters/ *Idhlaaq & ISmaat*			
4.6	L27-	Without Opposites- Whistling/ *Safeer*			
4.7	L27-	Without Opposites- Softness/ *Leen*			
4.8	L28-	Without Opposites- Repetition/ *Takreer*			
4.9	L29-	Without Opposites- Spreading/ *Tafashshi*			
4.10	L30-	Without Opposites- Elongation/ *IstiTaalah*			
4.11	L28-	Without Opposites- Deviation/ *Inhiraaf*			
4.12	L4-	Without Opposites- Bouncing/ *Qalqalah*			

Notes:

....
....
....
....
....
....
....

Suwar Annotation

❖ The main focus of this book is practising one's Qur'anic recitation and organising one's understanding of Tajweed rules.

❖ This section brings different suwar (plural of surah) of the noble Qur'an and expects the student to annotate any new rules discovered in that surah and continue doing so for the rest of the suwar until the rules are solidified.

❖ The aim is for the rules to be passive and for the recitation to be the main priority of the student's focus.

What Should Always be Annotated from the Beginning:

❖ Stretches should be clearly stated from the very beginning- 2 for a natural long vowel, 4 when a hamzah follows it and 6 when a sukoon or shaddah follows it. If one is stopping on a letter after a long vowel then the stretch should be 4 counts.

❖ Sukoon specialities should also be indicated every time- bouncy, continuous, clicky and half-stopping are good describers (when one learns the permanent qualities this will become much clearer, inshaa Allah).

Lesson 1- Surat Al Fatihah Part 1

- *Lesson focus*- Solidifying the throat letters- ء،ه ،ع ،ح ،غ ،خ *(2.1)*
- *Rule*- Laam Al Jalalah (the laam in the name of Allah) is light when a letter with kasrah precedes it *(3.1)*.

بِسْمِ اللَّهِ الرَّحْمَنِ الرَّحِيمِ ﴿١﴾

الْحَمْدُ لِلَّهِ رَبِّ الْعَالَمِينَ ﴿٢﴾ الرَّحْمَنِ الرَّحِيمِ ﴿٣﴾ مَلِكِ

يَوْمِ الدِّينِ ﴿٤﴾ إِيَّاكَ نَعْبُدُ وَإِيَّاكَ نَسْتَعِينُ ﴿٥﴾

Notes:

....

....

....

....

....

....

....

....

....

....

....

- o *Lesson focus*- Working on the exit points of ط and ض.
- o *Rule*- The sound continues in the <u>haa</u>, seen, ghayn and dhaad saakinah as does with many other letters *(4.2)*.

ٱهۡدِنَا

ٱلصِّرَطَ ٱلۡمُسۡتَقِيمَ ﴿٦﴾ صِرَطَ ٱلَّذِينَ أَنۡعَمۡتَ عَلَيۡهِمۡ غَيۡرِ ٱلۡمَغۡضُوبِ عَلَيۡهِمۡ وَلَا ٱلضَّآلِّينَ ﴿٧﴾

Notes:

....

....

....

....

....

....

....

....

....

....

....

- o *Lesson focus*- Differentiating the ء from the ع.
- o *Rule*- When there is a shaddah on the noon or meem, there will be nasalisation *(1.5)*.
- o *Rule*- When the Raa has a fathah or dhammah, it will be heavy *(3.2)*.

بِسْمِ ٱللَّهِ ٱلرَّحْمَٰنِ ٱلرَّحِيمِ

قُلْ أَعُوذُ بِرَبِّ ٱلنَّاسِ ﴿١﴾ مَلِكِ ٱلنَّاسِ ﴿٢﴾ إِلَٰهِ ٱلنَّاسِ ﴿٣﴾ مِن شَرِّ ٱلْوَسْوَاسِ ٱلْخَنَّاسِ ﴿٤﴾ ٱلَّذِى يُوَسْوِسُ فِ صُدُورِ ٱلنَّاسِ ﴿٥﴾ مِنَ ٱلْجِنَّةِ وَٱلنَّاسِ ﴿٦﴾

Notes:

....

....

....

....

....

....

....

....

....

....

- o *Lesson focus*- Articulating the qaaf with the correct bounce and keeping light letters light unaffected by the heavy letters (خ, ص, ض, غ, ط, ق, ظ).

- o *Rule*- When the Raa has a kasrah, it will be light *(3.2- complete)*.

- o *Rule*- When there is a permanent sukoon or a temporary sukoon (due to stopping) on the qaaf, TAA, baa, jeem and daal there will be a natural bounce (Qalqalah) *(4.12)*.

- o *Rule*- When any letter of the throat follows a noon saakinah or tanween, the noon saakinah or tanween will be clear (no extra nasalisation) as the throat letters are too distant for there to be any effect (Idh'haar) *(3.8 complete)*.

بِسْمِ اللَّهِ الرَّحْمَٰنِ الرَّحِيمِ

قُلْ أَعُوذُ بِرَبِّ ٱلْفَلَقِ ۝١ مِن شَرِّ مَا خَلَقَ ۝٢ وَمِن شَرِّ

غَاسِقٍ إِذَا وَقَبَ ۝٣ وَمِن شَرِّ ٱلنَّفَّٰثَٰتِ فِي ٱلْعُقَدِ ۝٤

وَمِن شَرِّ حَاسِدٍ إِذَا حَسَدَ ۝٥

Notes:

....

....

....

....

....

....

- o *Lesson focus*- Pronouncing the blessed name of Allah correctly.
- o *Rule*- Laam Al Jalalah (the laam in the name of Allah) is heavy when a letter with a dhammah or fathah precedes it *(3.1 completed)*.
- o *Rule*- When there is a laam or Raa after the noon saakinah/tanween, the noon saakinah/tanween will merge *completely (without nasalisation)* into that laam or raa.

  This is because the laam and Raa are very close to the noon in terms of exit point (Idghaam Kaamil) *(3.9)*.

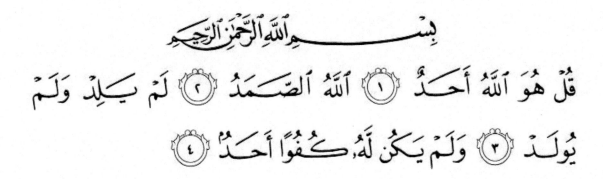

Notes:

....

....

....

....

....

....

....

....

- o *Lesson focus-* Getting used to nasalisation and the natural bounces.
- o *Rule-* Taa is a voiceless stopping letter. This means in sukoon a click is heard like a subtle puff of air *(4.1 & 4.2)*.
- o *Rule-* When there is a yaa, noon, meem or waw after the noon saakinah/tanween, the noon saakinah will merge *incompletely (with nasalisation)* into them as they are very close to the noon in terms of exit point (Idghaam Kaamil) *(3.9 complete)*.

بِسْمِ اللَّهِ الرَّحْمَٰنِ الرَّحِيمِ

تَبَّتْ يَدَآ أَبِى لَهَبٍ وَتَبَّ ۝ مَآ أَغْنَىٰ عَنْهُ مَالُهُۥ وَمَا

كَسَبَ ۝ سَيَصْلَىٰ نَارًا ذَاتَ لَهَبٍ ۝ وَٱمْرَأَتُهُۥ حَمَّالَةَ

ٱلْحَطَبِ ۝ فِى جِيدِهَا حَبْلٌ مِّن مَّسَدٍ ۝

Notes:

....

....

....

....

....

....

....

- o *Lesson focus*- Articulating the letter ص and ذ correctly.

- o *Rule*- If <u>one stops</u> on a letter with two fathahs, the two fathahs change into an alif, so we stretch 2 counts naturally upon stopping (Madd 'Iwadh) *(3.16)*.

بِسۡمِ ٱللَّهِ ٱلرَّحۡمَٰنِ ٱلرَّحِيمِ

إِذَا جَاءَ نَصۡرُ ٱللَّهِ وَٱلۡفَتۡحُ ﴿١﴾ وَرَأَيۡتَ ٱلنَّاسَ يَدۡخُلُونَ فِي دِينِ ٱللَّهِ أَفۡوَاجًا ﴿٢﴾ فَسَبِّحۡ بِحَمۡدِ رَبِّكَ وَٱسۡتَغۡفِرۡهُ إِنَّهُۥ كَانَ تَوَّابًا ﴿٣﴾

Notes:

....

....

....

....

....

....

....

....

....

Lesson 8- Surat Al Kafiroon

- o *Lesson focus*- Getting used to the 4 count stretches.
- o *Rule*- If there is a hamzah after a long vowel then one stretches the long vowel to 4 counts. Madd Muttasil (connected stretch) is when the hamzah is in the same word after the long vowel. Madd Munfasil (disconnected stretch) is when the hamzah is in the beginning of the next word after the long vowel *(3.13 complete)*.

- o Note: when an alif has an open circle like ٱ, it will only be pronounced when stopping and is otherwise silent.

بِسْمِ ٱللَّهِ ٱلرَّحْمَٰنِ ٱلرَّحِيمِ

قُلْ يَٰٓأَيُّهَا ٱلْكَٰفِرُونَ ﴿١﴾ لَآ أَعْبُدُ مَا تَعْبُدُونَ ﴿٢﴾ وَلَآ أَنتُمْ عَٰبِدُونَ مَآ أَعْبُدُ ﴿٣﴾ وَلَآ أَنَا۠ عَابِدٌ مَّا عَبَدتُّمْ ﴿٤﴾ وَلَآ أَنتُمْ عَٰبِدُونَ مَآ أَعْبُدُ ﴿٥﴾ لَكُمْ دِينُكُمْ وَلِيَ دِينِ ﴿٦﴾

Notes:

....

....

....

....

....

....

....

....

o *Lesson focus*- Practising the ع and ث.

o *Rule*- If the Raa is saakinah then it will be heavy if there is a fathah / alif long vowel or dhammah / waw long vowel preceding it *(3.3)*.

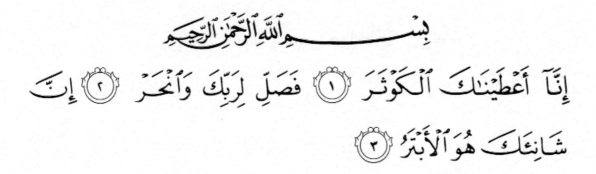

Notes:

....

....

....

....

....

....

....

....

....

....

....

- ○ *Lesson focus*- Practising the ع, ط and ض.
- ○ *Rule*- If the letter following is *not* from the throat letters (which are very far), or it is *not* from the merging letters (which are very close), then the noon saakinah or tanween will be hidden with a nasal sound whilst the tongue is near the exit point of the next letter (Ikhfaa) *(3.10 complete)*.

بِسْمِ اللَّهِ الرَّحْمَٰنِ الرَّحِيمِ

أَرَءَيْتَ الَّذِى يُكَذِّبُ بِالدِّينِ ﴿١﴾ فَذَٰلِكَ الَّذِى يَدُعُّ الْيَتِيمَ ﴿٢﴾ وَلَا يَحُضُّ عَلَىٰ طَعَامِ الْمِسْكِينِ ﴿٣﴾ فَوَيْلٌ لِّلْمُصَلِّينَ ﴿٤﴾ الَّذِينَ هُمْ عَن صَلَاتِهِمْ سَاهُونَ ﴿٥﴾ الَّذِينَ هُمْ يُرَاءُونَ ﴿٦﴾ وَيَمْنَعُونَ الْمَاعُونَ ﴿٧﴾

Notes:

....

....

....

....

....

....

....

....

o   *Lesson focus*- Balancing heavy letters and working on the letters ط and ع.

o   *Rule*- If after a meem saakinah there is another meem, both letters will merge together with a strong nasal sound (Idghaam Shafawi) *(3.5)*.

بِسْمِ اللَّهِ الرَّحْمَٰنِ الرَّحِيمِ

لِإِيلَٰفِ قُرَيْشٍ ﴿١﴾ إِۦلَٰفِهِمْ رِحْلَةَ الشِّتَآءِ وَالصَّيْفِ ﴿٢﴾

فَلْيَعْبُدُوا۟ رَبَّ هَٰذَا الْبَيْتِ ﴿٣﴾ الَّذِىٓ أَطْعَمَهُم مِّن جُوعٍ

وَءَامَنَهُم مِّنْ خَوْفٍ ﴿٤﴾

Notes:

....

....

....

....

....

....

....

....

....

....

Lesson 12- Surat Al Feel

- ○ *Lesson focus*- Working on the ص and ض saakinah.
- ○ *Rule*- If after a meem saakinah there is a baa, the meem saakinah will be hidden with an extended nasal sound (the lips must be closed) (ikhfaa shafawi) *(3.6)*.

بِسْمِ ٱللَّهِ ٱلرَّحْمَٰنِ ٱلرَّحِيمِ

أَلَمْ تَرَ كَيْفَ فَعَلَ رَبُّكَ بِأَصْحَابِ ٱلْفِيلِ ﴿١﴾ أَلَمْ يَجْعَلْ كَيْدَهُمْ فِي

تَضْلِيلٍ ﴿٢﴾ وَأَرْسَلَ عَلَيْهِمْ طَيْرًا أَبَابِيلَ ﴿٣﴾ تَرْمِيهِم بِحِجَارَةٍ

مِّن سِجِّيلٍ ﴿٤﴾ فَجَعَلَهُمْ كَعَصْفٍ مَّأْكُولٍ ﴿٥﴾

Notes:

....

....

....

....

....

....

....

....

....

o *Lesson focus*- Working on the heavy letters and perfecting the nasalisation where needed.

o *Rule*- If after a noon saakinah there is a baa, the noon saakinah will be changed into a meem saakinah (Iqlaab) due to the difficulty of nasalising it as a noon when there is a baa afterwards (*3.11 complete*).

o Once it changes to a meem saakinah, one refers to the rule of Ikhfaa Shafawi (mentioned in the previous lesson).

بِسْمِ اللَّهِ الرَّحْمَٰنِ الرَّحِيمِ

وَيْلٌ لِّكُلِّ هُمَزَةٍ لُّمَزَةٍ ﴿١﴾ الَّذِي جَمَعَ مَالًا وَعَدَّدَهُ ﴿٢﴾ يَحْسَبُ أَنَّ مَالَهُ أَخْلَدَهُ ﴿٣﴾ كَلَّا لَيُنبَذَنَّ فِي الْحُطَمَةِ ﴿٤﴾ وَمَا أَدْرَاكَ مَا الْحُطَمَةُ ﴿٥﴾ نَارُ اللَّهِ الْمُوقَدَةُ ﴿٦﴾ الَّتِي تَطَّلِعُ عَلَى الْأَفْئِدَةِ ﴿٧﴾ إِنَّهَا عَلَيْهِم مُّؤْصَدَةٌ ﴿٨﴾ فِي عَمَدٍ مُّمَدَّدَةٍ ﴿٩﴾

Notes:

....

....

....

....

....

....

....

....

- o *Lesson focus*- Balancing between heavy letters and light letters.
- o *Rule*- If the Raa is saakinah and before it is another saakinah, one looks at the vowelled letter before that. If that vowelled letter has a fathah or dhammah then the Raa saakinah will be heavy, if it has a kasrah then the Raa saakinah will be light *(3.3)*.

بِسْمِ اللَّهِ الرَّحْمَٰنِ الرَّحِيمِ

وَالْعَصْرِ ۝ إِنَّ الْإِنسَٰنَ لَفِي خُسْرٍ ۝ إِلَّا الَّذِينَ ءَامَنُوا۟ وَعَمِلُوا۟ الصَّٰلِحَٰتِ وَتَوَاصَوْا۟ بِالْحَقِّ وَتَوَاصَوْا۟ بِالصَّبْرِ ۝

Notes:

....

....

....

....

....

....

....

....

....

....

Lesson 15- Surat Al Takaathur

o *Lesson focus*- Practising the ر and working on the articulation of ع and ح.

o *Rule*- If the Raa is saakinah then it will be light if there is a kasrah / yaa saakinah preceding it
(3.3 complete).

بِسۡمِ ٱللَّهِ ٱلرَّحۡمَٰنِ ٱلرَّحِيمِ

أَلۡهَىٰكُمُ ٱلتَّكَاثُرُ ﴿١﴾ حَتَّىٰ زُرۡتُمُ ٱلۡمَقَابِرَ ﴿٢﴾ كَلَّا سَوۡفَ تَعۡلَمُونَ ﴿٣﴾ ثُمَّ كَلَّا سَوۡفَ تَعۡلَمُونَ ﴿٤﴾ كَلَّا لَوۡ تَعۡلَمُونَ عِلۡمَ ٱلۡيَقِينِ ﴿٥﴾ لَتَرَوُنَّ ٱلۡجَحِيمَ ﴿٦﴾ ثُمَّ لَتَرَوُنَّهَا عَيۡنَ ٱلۡيَقِينِ ﴿٧﴾ ثُمَّ لَتُسۡـَٔلُنَّ يَوۡمَئِذٍ عَنِ ٱلنَّعِيمِ ﴿٨﴾

Notes:

....

....

....

....

....

....

....

....

- o *Lesson focus-* Differentiating ه from the ع.
- o *Rule-* Consolidating previous rules.

بِسْمِ ٱللَّهِ ٱلرَّحْمَٰنِ ٱلرَّحِيمِ

ٱلْقَارِعَةُ ﴿١﴾ مَا ٱلْقَارِعَةُ ﴿٢﴾ وَمَآ أَدْرَىٰكَ مَا ٱلْقَارِعَةُ ﴿٣﴾ يَوْمَ يَكُونُ ٱلنَّاسُ كَٱلْفَرَاشِ ٱلْمَبْثُوثِ ﴿٤﴾ وَتَكُونُ ٱلْجِبَالُ كَٱلْعِهْنِ ٱلْمَنفُوشِ ﴿٥﴾ فَأَمَّا مَن ثَقُلَتْ مَوَٰزِينُهُۥ ﴿٦﴾ فَهُوَ فِي عِيشَةٍ رَّاضِيَةٍ ﴿٧﴾ وَأَمَّا مَنْ خَفَّتْ مَوَٰزِينُهُۥ ﴿٨﴾ فَأُمُّهُۥ هَاوِيَةٌ ﴿٩﴾ وَمَآ أَدْرَىٰكَ مَا هِيَهْ ﴿١٠﴾ نَارٌ حَامِيَةٌۢ ﴿١١﴾

Notes:

....

....

....

....

....

....

....

o *Lesson focus*- Balancing heavy and light letters/ making the bouncy letters clear.

o *Rule*- Most of the time, the haa at the end of a word (with kasrah or dhammah) is the masculine pronoun.

o If this haa has a vowelled letter <u>before</u> and <u>after</u> it, it will be stretched naturally to 2 counts (madd silah sughraa- the small joining stretch).

o If there is a hamzah after it, the stretch will be 4 counts (madd silah kubraa- the big joining stretch) *(3.15)*.

بِسْمِ ٱللَّهِ ٱلرَّحْمَٰنِ ٱلرَّحِيمِ

وَٱلْعَٰدِيَٰتِ ضَبْحًا ﴿١﴾ فَٱلْمُورِيَٰتِ قَدْحًا ﴿٢﴾ فَٱلْمُغِيرَٰتِ صُبْحًا ﴿٣﴾

فَأَثَرْنَ بِهِۦ نَقْعًا ﴿٤﴾ فَوَسَطْنَ بِهِۦ جَمْعًا ﴿٥﴾ إِنَّ ٱلْإِنسَٰنَ لِرَبِّهِۦ لَكَنُودٌ

﴿٦﴾ وَإِنَّهُۥ عَلَىٰ ذَٰلِكَ لَشَهِيدٌ ﴿٧﴾ وَإِنَّهُۥ لِحُبِّ ٱلْخَيْرِ لَشَدِيدٌ ﴿٨﴾

أَفَلَا يَعْلَمُ إِذَا بُعْثِرَ مَا فِي ٱلْقُبُورِ ﴿٩﴾ وَحُصِّلَ مَا فِي ٱلصُّدُورِ ﴿١٠﴾ إِنَّ

رَبَّهُم بِهِمْ يَوْمَئِذٍ لَّخَبِيرٌ ﴿١١﴾

Notes:

………………………………………………………………………………………

………………………………………………………………………………………

………………………………………………………………………………………

………………………………………………………………………………………

………………………………………………………………………………………

- *Lesson focus-* Perfecting all letters and working on giving the appropriate time to letters in sukoon.
- *Rule-* The khaa, sheen and thaa are from amongst the continuous letters *(4.2)*.

بِسْمِ اللَّهِ الرَّحْمَٰنِ الرَّحِيمِ

إِذَا زُلْزِلَتِ ٱلْأَرْضُ زِلْزَالَهَا ﴿١﴾ وَأَخْرَجَتِ ٱلْأَرْضُ أَثْقَالَهَا ﴿٢﴾

وَقَالَ ٱلْإِنسَٰنُ مَا لَهَا ﴿٣﴾ يَوْمَئِذٍ تُحَدِّثُ أَخْبَارَهَا ﴿٤﴾ بِأَنَّ رَبَّكَ

أَوْحَىٰ لَهَا ﴿٥﴾ يَوْمَئِذٍ يَصْدُرُ ٱلنَّاسُ أَشْتَاتًا لِّيُرَوْا۟ أَعْمَٰلَهُمْ

﴿٦﴾ فَمَن يَعْمَلْ مِثْقَالَ ذَرَّةٍ خَيْرًا يَرَهُۥ ﴿٧﴾ وَمَن يَعْمَلْ

مِثْقَالَ ذَرَّةٍ شَرًّا يَرَهُۥ ﴿٨﴾

Notes:

....

....

....

....

....

....

....

o *Lesson focus*- Perfecting all letters and consolidating the practise of rules previously learnt.

بِسْمِ ٱللَّهِ ٱلرَّحْمَٰنِ ٱلرَّحِيمِ

لَمْ يَكُنِ ٱلَّذِينَ كَفَرُوا۟ مِنْ أَهْلِ ٱلْكِتَٰبِ وَٱلْمُشْرِكِينَ مُنفَكِّينَ حَتَّىٰ تَأْتِيَهُمُ

ٱلْبَيِّنَةُ ﴿١﴾ رَسُولٌ مِّنَ ٱللَّهِ يَتْلُوا۟ صُحُفًا مُّطَهَّرَةً ﴿٢﴾ فِيهَا كُتُبٌ قَيِّمَةٌ

﴿٣﴾ وَمَا تَفَرَّقَ ٱلَّذِينَ أُوتُوا۟ ٱلْكِتَٰبَ إِلَّا مِنۢ بَعْدِ مَا جَآءَتْهُمُ ٱلْبَيِّنَةُ ﴿٤﴾

وَمَآ أُمِرُوٓا۟ إِلَّا لِيَعْبُدُوا۟ ٱللَّهَ مُخْلِصِينَ لَهُ ٱلدِّينَ حُنَفَآءَ وَيُقِيمُوا۟ ٱلصَّلَوٰةَ

وَيُؤْتُوا۟ ٱلزَّكَوٰةَ وَذَٰلِكَ دِينُ ٱلْقَيِّمَةِ ﴿٥﴾ إِنَّ ٱلَّذِينَ كَفَرُوا۟ مِنْ أَهْلِ

ٱلْكِتَٰبِ وَٱلْمُشْرِكِينَ فِى نَارِ جَهَنَّمَ خَٰلِدِينَ فِيهَآ أُو۟لَٰٓئِكَ هُمْ شَرُّ ٱلْبَرِيَّةِ

﴿٦﴾ إِنَّ ٱلَّذِينَ ءَامَنُوا۟ وَعَمِلُوا۟ ٱلصَّٰلِحَٰتِ أُو۟لَٰٓئِكَ هُمْ خَيْرُ ٱلْبَرِيَّةِ

﴿٧﴾ جَزَآؤُهُمْ عِندَ رَبِّهِمْ جَنَّٰتُ عَدْنٍ تَجْرِى مِن تَحْتِهَا ٱلْأَنْهَٰرُ خَٰلِدِينَ

فِيهَآ أَبَدًا رَّضِىَ ٱللَّهُ عَنْهُمْ وَرَضُوا۟ عَنْهُ ذَٰلِكَ لِمَنْ خَشِىَ رَبَّهُۥ ﴿٨﴾

Notes:

....

....

....

....

....

o *Lesson focus-* Working on the heavy Raa saakinah and ensuring light letters remain light.

o *Rule-* the haa and dhaal are from the continuous letters *(4.2)*.

بِسْمِ اللَّهِ الرَّحْمَٰنِ الرَّحِيمِ

إِنَّآ أَنزَلْنَٰهُ فِى لَيْلَةِ ٱلْقَدْرِ ﴿١﴾ وَمَآ أَدْرَىٰكَ مَا لَيْلَةُ ٱلْقَدْرِ ﴿٢﴾ لَيْلَةُ ٱلْقَدْرِ خَيْرٌ مِّنْ أَلْفِ شَهْرٍ ﴿٣﴾ تَنَزَّلُ ٱلْمَلَٰٓئِكَةُ وَٱلرُّوحُ فِيهَا بِإِذْنِ رَبِّهِم مِّن كُلِّ أَمْرٍ ﴿٤﴾ سَلَٰمٌ هِىَ حَتَّىٰ مَطْلَعِ ٱلْفَجْرِ ﴿٥﴾

Notes:

....

....

....

....

....

....

....

....

....

o *Lesson focus*- Preserving light letters whilst maintaining heavy letters. Also preserving long vowels.

o *Rule*- If after a meem saakinah there is *any* letter *other than* the baa or meem then it will be clear without any extra nasal sound (Idh'haar Shafawi) *(3.7 complete)*.

بِسْمِ اللَّهِ الرَّحْمَٰنِ الرَّحِيمِ

اقْرَأْ بِاسْمِ رَبِّكَ الَّذِي خَلَقَ ﴿١﴾ خَلَقَ الْإِنسَانَ مِنْ عَلَقٍ ﴿٢﴾ اقْرَأْ وَرَبُّكَ الْأَكْرَمُ ﴿٣﴾ الَّذِي عَلَّمَ بِالْقَلَمِ ﴿٤﴾ عَلَّمَ الْإِنسَانَ مَا لَمْ يَعْلَمْ ﴿٥﴾ كَلَّا إِنَّ الْإِنسَانَ لَيَطْغَىٰ ﴿٦﴾ أَن رَّآهُ اسْتَغْنَىٰ ﴿٧﴾ إِنَّ إِلَىٰ رَبِّكَ الرُّجْعَىٰ ﴿٨﴾ أَرَأَيْتَ الَّذِي يَنْهَىٰ ﴿٩﴾ عَبْدًا إِذَا صَلَّىٰ ﴿١٠﴾ أَرَأَيْتَ إِن كَانَ عَلَى الْهُدَىٰ ﴿١١﴾ أَوْ أَمَرَ بِالتَّقْوَىٰ ﴿١٢﴾ أَرَأَيْتَ إِن كَذَّبَ وَتَوَلَّىٰ ﴿١٣﴾ أَلَمْ يَعْلَم بِأَنَّ اللَّهَ يَرَىٰ ﴿١٤﴾ كَلَّا لَئِن لَّمْ يَنتَهِ لَنَسْفَعًا بِالنَّاصِيَةِ ﴿١٥﴾ نَاصِيَةٍ كَاذِبَةٍ خَاطِئَةٍ ﴿١٦﴾ فَلْيَدْعُ نَادِيَهُ ﴿١٧﴾ سَنَدْعُ الزَّبَانِيَةَ ﴿١٨﴾ كَلَّا لَا تُطِعْهُ وَاسْجُدْ وَاقْتَرِب ۩ ﴿١٩﴾

Notes:

....

....

....

....

....

o *Lesson focus*- Preserving light letters whilst maintaining heavy letters. Also preserving long vowels.

o *Rule*- If one is stopping on a letter (causing that letter to temporarily become saakinah) after a long vowel then the long vowel maybe stretched 2, 4 or 6 counts. 4 counts are optimal. (Madd 'Aaridh) *(3.15 complete).*

بِسْمِ اللَّهِ الرَّحْمَٰنِ الرَّحِيمِ

وَالتِّينِ وَالزَّيْتُونِ ﴿١﴾ وَطُورِ سِينِينَ ﴿٢﴾ وَهَٰذَا الْبَلَدِ الْأَمِينِ ﴿٣﴾ لَقَدْ خَلَقْنَا الْإِنسَٰنَ فِي أَحْسَنِ تَقْوِيمٍ ﴿٤﴾ ثُمَّ رَدَدْنَٰهُ أَسْفَلَ سَٰفِلِينَ ﴿٥﴾ إِلَّا الَّذِينَ ءَامَنُوا وَعَمِلُوا الصَّٰلِحَٰتِ فَلَهُمْ أَجْرٌ غَيْرُ مَمْنُونٍ ﴿٦﴾ فَمَا يُكَذِّبُكَ بَعْدُ بِالدِّينِ ﴿٧﴾ أَلَيْسَ اللَّهُ بِأَحْكَمِ الْحَٰكِمِينَ ﴿٨﴾

Notes:

....

....

....

....

....

....

....

....

o *Lesson focus*- Preserving light letters whilst maintaining heavy letters. Being careful upon *ikhfaa* when there is a heavy letter afterwards.

o *Rule*- Remember, the sheen, 7haa, zaa, seen, ghayn and haa are from the continuous letters (the sound will continue) *(4.2)*.

o *Rule*- The kaaf saakinah will be clicked as it is a voiceless stopping letter *(4.1)*.

بِسْمِ ٱللَّهِ ٱلرَّحْمَٰنِ ٱلرَّحِيمِ

أَلَمْ نَشْرَحْ لَكَ صَدْرَكَ ﴿١﴾ وَوَضَعْنَا عَنكَ وِزْرَكَ ﴿٢﴾ ٱلَّذِىٓ أَنقَضَ ظَهْرَكَ ﴿٣﴾ وَرَفَعْنَا لَكَ ذِكْرَكَ ﴿٤﴾ فَإِنَّ مَعَ ٱلْعُسْرِ يُسْرًا ﴿٥﴾ إِنَّ مَعَ ٱلْعُسْرِ يُسْرًا ﴿٦﴾ فَإِذَا فَرَغْتَ فَٱنصَبْ ﴿٧﴾ وَإِلَىٰ رَبِّكَ فَٱرْغَب ﴿٨﴾

Notes:

....

....

....

....

....

....

....

....

....

o *Lesson focus*- Perfecting the stretches.

o *Rule*- If there is a sukoon or shaddah after the long vowel then one stretches to 6 counts (Madd Laazim) *(3.14)*.

o *Rule*- If there is a hamzah before a long vowel then it is still a natural prolongation in essence; however, it is called an "exchanged stretch" (Madd Badal) *(3.16 complete)*.

o This is because the long vowel came in exchange of a second hamzah that was after the first hamzah (the second hamzah was changed to a corresponding long vowel).

o Remember, long vowels are a) alif after a fathah b) yaa saakinah after a kasrah c) waw saakinah after a dhammah (Madd Asli) (2 counts) *(3.12)*.

بِسْمِ ٱللَّهِ ٱلرَّحْمَٰنِ ٱلرَّحِيمِ

وَٱلضُّحَىٰ ﴿١﴾ وَٱلَّيْلِ إِذَا سَجَىٰ ﴿٢﴾ مَا وَدَّعَكَ رَبُّكَ وَمَا قَلَىٰ ﴿٣﴾ وَلَلْأَخِرَةُ خَيْرٌ لَّكَ مِنَ ٱلْأُولَىٰ ﴿٤﴾ وَلَسَوْفَ يُعْطِيكَ رَبُّكَ فَتَرْضَىٰ ﴿٥﴾ أَلَمْ يَجِدْكَ يَتِيمًا فَـَٔاوَىٰ ﴿٦﴾ وَوَجَدَكَ ضَآلًّا فَهَدَىٰ ﴿٧﴾ وَوَجَدَكَ عَآئِلًا فَأَغْنَىٰ ﴿٨﴾ فَأَمَّا ٱلْيَتِيمَ فَلَا تَقْهَرْ ﴿٩﴾ وَأَمَّا ٱلسَّآئِلَ فَلَا تَنْهَرْ ﴿١٠﴾ وَأَمَّا بِنِعْمَةِ رَبِّكَ فَحَدِّثْ ﴿١١﴾

Notes:

....

....

o *Lesson focus*- Perfecting the pronunciation of the letters in sukoon.

o *Rule*- Certain letters are voiced (Jahr) (the vocal cords vibrate upon articulation) whilst others are voiceless (Hams) (the vocal cords do not vibrate) *(4.1 complete)*.

- If vibration is felt in the throat during pronunciation, then the letter is likely to be voiced; if there is no vibration and air can be felt on the palm then the letter is likely to be voiceless.

- The voiceless letters are فحثه شخص سكت. The rest are voiced.

o *Rule*- Certain letters have continuous sounds (Rikhaawah) and certain letters have stopping sounds (Shiddah). Some letters have both an element of stopping and continuation (TawassuT) *(4.2 complete)*.

- If air can pass through the exit point, the letter is considered to be continuous (all other letters).

- If air cannot pass through then they are stopping letters (أجد قط بكت).

- If air stops at the exit point but continues through another pathway then they are in the middle of being stopping and continuous (لن عمر).

47

o *Lesson focus*- Perfecting the heavy letters.

o *Rule*- Certain letters are considered to be "heavy"- the back of the tongue rises to the soft palate

   upon articulation (Isti'laa') (خص ضغط قظ).

   Other letters are considered to be "light"- the back of the tongue doesn't rise upon articulation
   (Istifaal) (all other letters) *(4.3 complete)*.

o *Rule*- Certain letters are considered to be "closed/adhered"- the middle of the tongue rises

   towards the palate upon articulation (Itbaaq) (ص ض ط ظ). Note- these letters are also
   "heavy".

   Other letters are considered to be "open"- the middle of the tongue doesn't rise upon articulation-
   it is as if there is more of an opening in the middle of the tongue (Infitaa<u>h</u>)) (all other letters) *(4.4*

   complete).

o *Rule*- Certain letters are considered "fluent" (فر من لب) (idhlaaq) others are considered as being

   "hindered" (all other letters) (ISmaat). This has no *Tajweed* bearing but is of grammatical

   importance *(4.5 complete)*.

بِسۡمِ ٱللَّهِ ٱلرَّحۡمَٰنِ ٱلرَّحِيمِ

وَٱلشَّمۡسِ وَضُحَىٰهَا ﴿١﴾ وَٱلۡقَمَرِ إِذَا تَلَىٰهَا ﴿٢﴾ وَٱلنَّهَارِ إِذَا جَلَّىٰهَا ﴿٣﴾ وَٱلَّيۡلِ

إِذَا يَغۡشَىٰهَا ﴿٤﴾ وَٱلسَّمَآءِ وَمَا بَنَىٰهَا ﴿٥﴾ وَٱلۡأَرۡضِ وَمَا طَحَىٰهَا ﴿٦﴾ وَنَفۡسٍ

وَمَا سَوَّىٰهَا ﴿٧﴾ فَأَلۡهَمَهَا فُجُورَهَا وَتَقۡوَىٰهَا ﴿٨﴾ قَدۡ أَفۡلَحَ مَن زَكَّىٰهَا ﴿٩﴾

وَقَدۡ خَابَ مَن دَسَّىٰهَا ﴿١٠﴾ كَذَّبَتۡ ثَمُودُ بِطَغۡوَىٰهَآ ﴿١١﴾ إِذِ ٱنۢبَعَثَ

أَشۡقَىٰهَا ﴿١٢﴾ فَقَالَ لَهُمۡ رَسُولُ ٱللَّهِ نَاقَةَ ٱللَّهِ وَسُقۡيَٰهَا ﴿١٣﴾

فَكَذَّبُوهُ فَعَقَرُوهَا فَدَمۡدَمَ عَلَيۡهِمۡ رَبُّهُم بِذَنۢبِهِمۡ فَسَوَّىٰهَا

﴿١٤﴾ وَلَا يَخَافُ عُقۡبَٰهَا ﴿١٥﴾

o *Lesson focus*- Perfecting the noon saakinah rules.

o *Rule*- Seen, Saad and Zaa are all "whistling" letters (Safeer). Due to tightness in the exit point, the air passing makes a sound that resembles a whistle or a buzz *(4.6 complete)*.

o *Rule*- Yaa and waw have the quality of "softness" (Leen). When they are saakinah and preceded by a fathah, there is a smooth transition into these letters- for example, "aw" and "ay" (this is called a diphthong in English) *(4.7 complete)*.

بِسْمِ اللَّهِ الرَّحْمَٰنِ الرَّحِيمِ

لَا أُقْسِمُ بِهَٰذَا الْبَلَدِ ﴿١﴾ وَأَنتَ حِلٌّ بِهَٰذَا الْبَلَدِ ﴿٢﴾ وَوَالِدٍ وَمَا وَلَدَ ﴿٣﴾ لَقَدْ خَلَقْنَا الْإِنسَٰنَ فِي كَبَدٍ ﴿٤﴾ أَيَحْسَبُ أَن لَّن يَقْدِرَ عَلَيْهِ أَحَدٌ ﴿٥﴾ يَقُولُ أَهْلَكْتُ مَالًا لُّبَدًا ﴿٦﴾ أَيَحْسَبُ أَن لَّمْ يَرَهُ أَحَدٌ ﴿٧﴾ أَلَمْ نَجْعَل لَّهُ عَيْنَيْنِ ﴿٨﴾ وَلِسَانًا وَشَفَتَيْنِ ﴿٩﴾ وَهَدَيْنَاهُ النَّجْدَيْنِ ﴿١٠﴾

Notes:

....

....

....

....

....

....

- o *Lesson focus*- Perfecting the noon saakinah rules and perfecting the Raa.
- o *Rule*- The Raa has a special quality of repetition (Takreer). This is due to tightness in the exit point and the passing air causing the tongue to "frap" due to pressure. One should try not to exaggerate this quality, rather it should be kept under control *(4.8 complete)*.
- o *Rule*- Both the Raa and Laam have the quality of "drifting" or "deviation" (Inḥiraaf). This is because the air drifts through a secondary passageway after arriving at the exit point. Air passes through the sides for the laam and through a small hole at the tip of the tongue for the Raa *(4.11 complete)*.

فَلَا ٱقْتَحَمَ

ٱلْعَقَبَةَ ﴿١١﴾ وَمَآ أَدْرَىٰكَ مَا ٱلْعَقَبَةُ ﴿١٢﴾ فَكُّ رَقَبَةٍ ﴿١٣﴾ أَوْ إِطْعَـٰمٌ فِي يَوْمٍ

ذِى مَسْغَبَةٍ ﴿١٤﴾ يَتِيمًا ذَا مَقْرَبَةٍ ﴿١٥﴾ أَوْ مِسْكِينًا ذَا مَتْرَبَةٍ ﴿١٦﴾ ثُمَّ كَانَ

مِنَ ٱلَّذِينَ ءَامَنُوا۟ وَتَوَاصَوْا۟ بِٱلصَّبْرِ وَتَوَاصَوْا۟ بِٱلْمَرْحَمَةِ ﴿١٧﴾ أُو۟لَـٰٓئِكَ أَصْحَـٰبُ

ٱلْمَيْمَنَةِ ﴿١٨﴾ وَٱلَّذِينَ كَفَرُوا۟ بِـَٔايَـٰتِنَا هُمْ أَصْحَـٰبُ ٱلْمَشْـَٔمَةِ ﴿١٩﴾ عَلَيْهِمْ نَارٌ

مُّؤْصَدَةٌۢ ﴿٢٠﴾

Notes:

....

....

....

....

o *Lesson focus*- Perfecting the rules of the letter Raa.

o *Rule*- The sheen has a special quality of "spreading" (Tafashshi). This is because air freely spreads through mouth due to a absence of tightness *(4.9 complete)*.

o *Rule*- Usually, if a kasrah precedes a Raa saakinah then the Raa saakinah will be light. However, there are two exceptions *(3.4)*.

- Exception 1: If the Raa saakinah is preceded by a kasrah but has a heavy letter afterwards the Raa saakinah will still be heavy (and not light). An example is in the portion below.

بِسْمِ اللَّهِ الرَّحْمَٰنِ الرَّحِيمِ

وَالْفَجْرِ ﴿١﴾ وَلَيَالٍ عَشْرٍ ﴿٢﴾ وَالشَّفْعِ وَالْوَتْرِ ﴿٣﴾ وَاللَّيْلِ إِذَا يَسْرِ ﴿٤﴾ هَلْ فِي ذَٰلِكَ قَسَمٌ لِّذِي حِجْرٍ ﴿٥﴾ أَلَمْ تَرَ كَيْفَ فَعَلَ رَبُّكَ بِعَادٍ ﴿٦﴾ إِرَمَ ذَاتِ الْعِمَادِ ﴿٧﴾ الَّتِي لَمْ يُخْلَقْ مِثْلُهَا فِي الْبِلَادِ ﴿٨﴾ وَثَمُودَ الَّذِينَ جَابُوا الصَّخْرَ بِالْوَادِ ﴿٩﴾ وَفِرْعَوْنَ ذِي الْأَوْتَادِ ﴿١٠﴾ الَّذِينَ طَغَوْا فِي الْبِلَادِ ﴿١١﴾ فَأَكْثَرُوا فِيهَا الْفَسَادَ ﴿١٢﴾ فَصَبَّ عَلَيْهِمْ رَبُّكَ سَوْطَ عَذَابٍ ﴿١٣﴾ إِنَّ رَبَّكَ لَبِالْمِرْصَادِ ﴿١٤﴾ فَأَمَّا الْإِنسَانُ إِذَا مَا ابْتَلَاهُ رَبُّهُ فَأَكْرَمَهُ وَنَعَّمَهُ فَيَقُولُ رَبِّي أَكْرَمَنِ ﴿١٥﴾ وَأَمَّا إِذَا مَا ابْتَلَاهُ فَقَدَرَ عَلَيْهِ رِزْقَهُ فَيَقُولُ رَبِّي أَهَانَنِ ﴿١٦﴾

Notes:

……………………………………………………………………………………………

……………………………………………………………………………………………

o *Lesson focus*- Perfecting the rules of the letter Raa.

o *Rule*- The Dhaad has a special quality of elongation (IstiTaalah). This is because the Dhaad has the longest exit point- the side of tongue along the edges of the upper molar teeth. This causes a type of gliding of the tongue until it reaches the exit point of the Dhaa (if held long enough) *(4.10 complete)*.

o *Rule*- Usually, if a kasrah precedes a Raa saakinah then the Raa saakinah will be light. However, there are two exceptions *(3.4 complete)*.

- Exception 2: If the Raa saakinah is preceded by a kasrah but the kasrah is temporary- due to being on a joining hamzah (an example is in the portion below).

- Also, the kasrah maybe temporary if it was placed to connect a letter that was saakinah onto another saakinah letter. The example of this is أَمِ ارْتَابوا - this was originally أَمْ ارْتَابوا but the meem saakinah couldn't join onto the Raa saakinah, so a kasrah was presented to facilitate the transition.

كَلَّا بَل لَّا تُكْرِمُونَ ٱلْيَتِيمَ ﴿١٧﴾ وَلَا تَحَٰضُّونَ عَلَىٰ

طَعَامِ ٱلْمِسْكِينِ ﴿١٨﴾ وَتَأْكُلُونَ ٱلتُّرَاثَ أَكْلًا لَّمًّا ﴿١٩﴾

وَتُحِبُّونَ ٱلْمَالَ حُبًّا جَمًّا ﴿٢٠﴾ كَلَّا إِذَا دُكَّتِ ٱلْأَرْضُ دَكًّا دَكًّا ﴿٢١﴾

وَجَاءَ رَبُّكَ وَٱلْمَلَكُ صَفًّا صَفًّا ﴿٢٢﴾ وَجِائَئَ يَوْمَئِذٍ بِجَهَنَّمَ يَوْمَئِذٍ

يَتَذَكَّرُ ٱلْإِنسَٰنُ وَأَنَّىٰ لَهُ ٱلذِّكْرَىٰ ﴿٢٣﴾ يَقُولُ يَٰلَيْتَنِي قَدَّمْتُ لِحَيَاتِي

﴿٢٤﴾ فَيَوْمَئِذٍ لَّا يُعَذِّبُ عَذَابَهُ أَحَدٌ ﴿٢٥﴾ وَلَا يُوثِقُ وَثَاقَهُ أَحَدٌ ﴿٢٦﴾ يَٰأَيَّتُهَا

ٱلنَّفْسُ ٱلْمُطْمَئِنَّةُ ﴿٢٧﴾ ٱرْجِعِي إِلَىٰ رَبِّكِ رَاضِيَةً مَّرْضِيَّةً ﴿٢٨﴾ فَٱدْخُلِي فِي عِبَٰدِي

﴿٢٩﴾ وَٱدْخُلِي جَنَّتِي ﴿٣٠﴾

:

o *Lesson focus*- Focusing on correct pronunciation and application of all rules learnt thus far.

o *Rule*- Merging (Idghaam) between two letters sometimes occurs during Qur'anic recitation in order to bring ease and facilitation.

o The majority of the time, the <u>first letter is saakinah</u> and <u>the second is vowelled</u> (muta*h*arrikah)- if merging happens like this it is called a <u>minor merging</u> (Idghaam Sagheer). Remember, a tanween ends with a noon saakinah (recall the instances of merging in the noon saakinah chapter) *(3.17 complete)*.

بِسْمِ اللَّهِ الرَّحْمَٰنِ الرَّحِيمِ

هَلْ أَتَىٰكَ حَدِيثُ الْغَٰشِيَةِ ﴿١﴾ وُجُوهٌ يَوْمَئِذٍ خَٰشِعَةٌ ﴿٢﴾ عَامِلَةٌ

نَّاصِبَةٌ ﴿٣﴾ تَصْلَىٰ نَارًا حَامِيَةً ﴿٤﴾ تُسْقَىٰ مِنْ عَيْنٍ ءَانِيَةٍ ﴿٥﴾ لَّيْسَ لَهُمْ طَعَامٌ

إِلَّا مِن ضَرِيعٍ ﴿٦﴾ لَّا يُسْمِنُ وَلَا يُغْنِى مِن جُوعٍ ﴿٧﴾ وُجُوهٌ يَوْمَئِذٍ نَّاعِمَةٌ

﴿٨﴾ لِّسَعْيِهَا رَاضِيَةٌ ﴿٩﴾ فِى جَنَّةٍ عَالِيَةٍ ﴿١٠﴾ لَّا تَسْمَعُ فِيهَا لَٰغِيَةً ﴿١١﴾ فِيهَا

عَيْنٌ جَارِيَةٌ ﴿١٢﴾ فِيهَا سُرُرٌ مَّرْفُوعَةٌ ﴿١٣﴾ وَأَكْوَابٌ مَّوْضُوعَةٌ ﴿١٤﴾ وَنَمَارِقُ

مَصْفُوفَةٌ ﴿١٥﴾ وَزَرَابِيُّ مَبْثُوثَةٌ ﴿١٦﴾

Notes:

....

....

....

....

o *Lesson focus*- Focusing on correct pronunciation and application of all rules learnt thus far.

o *Rule*- Merging (Idghaam) between two letters sometimes occurs during Qur'anic recitation in order to bring ease and facilitation.

o Rarely, the <u>first letter is vowelled</u> and the <u>second letter is also vowelled</u>. If merging occurs like this then this is called a <u>major merging</u> (Idghaam Kabeer). There are only a few examples in the whole Qur'an for this- one cannot see the two letters merging as they have already been unified with a *shaddah* in the written script *(3.18 complete)*.

o The instances of Idghaam Kabeer- لَاتَأۡمَنَّا (Yusuf: 11) | مَكَّنِّي (Al Kahf: 95) | أَتُحَـٰجُّوٓنِّي (Al An'aam: 80) | تَأۡمُرُوٓنِّي (Az Zumar: 64) | فَنِعِمَّا (Al Baqarah: 271)

o لَاتَأۡمَنَّا is a special occurrence. It was originally: تَأۡمُنُنَا. It is important to show that the dhammah was once there- hence, one should 1) round their lips as they pronounce the noon with shaddah and fathah or 2) do a quick dhammah (about 2/3 its normal length) and then pronounce the second noon with fathah normally. A teacher's demonstration is essential to grasp this.

أَفَلَا يَنظُرُونَ إِلَى ٱلۡإِبِلِ كَيۡفَ خُلِقَتۡ ۝ وَإِلَى ٱلسَّمَآءِ كَيۡفَ رُفِعَتۡ ۝ وَإِلَى ٱلۡجِبَالِ كَيۡفَ نُصِبَتۡ ۝ وَإِلَى ٱلۡأَرۡضِ كَيۡفَ سُطِحَتۡ ۝ فَذَكِّرۡ إِنَّمَآ أَنتَ مُذَكِّرٌ ۝ لَّسۡتَ عَلَيۡهِم بِمُصَيۡطِرٍ ۝ إِلَّا مَن تَوَلَّىٰ وَكَفَرَ ۝ فَيُعَذِّبُهُ ٱللَّهُ ٱلۡعَذَابَ ٱلۡأَكۡبَرَ ۝ إِنَّ إِلَيۡنَآ إِيَابَهُمۡ ۝ ثُمَّ إِنَّ عَلَيۡنَا حِسَابَهُم ۝

o *Lesson focus*- Focusing on correct pronunciation and application of all rules learnt thus far.

o *Rule*- Letters have different relationships with the letters that follow them. Sometimes this can lead to a merging based on the level of closeness the letter has with the next letter.

o When two letters that are <u>absolutely identical meet</u>, <u>the first being saakinah</u> and <u>the second being vowelled</u>, the first will *<u>always</u>* be merged into the second. This is a minor merging of two identical letters (Idghaam Mutamaathilayn Sagheer) *(3.19 complete)*.

بِسْمِ اللَّهِ الرَّحْمَٰنِ الرَّحِيمِ

سَبِّحِ اسْمَ رَبِّكَ الْأَعْلَى ﴿١﴾ الَّذِي خَلَقَ فَسَوَّىٰ ﴿٢﴾ وَالَّذِي قَدَّرَ فَهَدَىٰ ﴿٣﴾

وَالَّذِي أَخْرَجَ الْمَرْعَىٰ ﴿٤﴾ فَجَعَلَهُ غُثَاءً أَحْوَىٰ ﴿٥﴾ سَنُقْرِئُكَ فَلَا تَنسَىٰ ﴿٦﴾

إِلَّا مَا شَاءَ اللَّهُ إِنَّهُ يَعْلَمُ الْجَهْرَ وَمَا يَخْفَىٰ ﴿٧﴾ وَنُيَسِّرُكَ لِلْيُسْرَىٰ ﴿٨﴾ فَذَكِّرْ

إِن نَّفَعَتِ الذِّكْرَىٰ ﴿٩﴾ سَيَذَّكَّرُ مَن يَخْشَىٰ ﴿١٠﴾ وَيَتَجَنَّبُهَا الْأَشْقَى ﴿١١﴾

الَّذِي يَصْلَى النَّارَ الْكُبْرَىٰ ﴿١٢﴾ ثُمَّ لَا يَمُوتُ فِيهَا وَلَا يَحْيَىٰ ﴿١٣﴾ قَدْ أَفْلَحَ مَن

تَزَكَّىٰ ﴿١٤﴾ وَذَكَرَ اسْمَ رَبِّهِ فَصَلَّىٰ ﴿١٥﴾ بَلْ تُؤْثِرُونَ الْحَيَاةَ الدُّنْيَا ﴿١٦﴾

وَالْآخِرَةُ خَيْرٌ وَأَبْقَىٰ ﴿١٧﴾ إِنَّ هَٰذَا لَفِي الصُّحُفِ الْأُولَىٰ ﴿١٨﴾ صُحُفِ

إِبْرَاهِيمَ وَمُوسَىٰ ﴿١٩﴾

Notes:

....

....

....

o *Lesson focus-* Focusing on correct pronunciation and application of all rules learnt thus far.

o *Rule-* Letters have different relationships with the letters that follow them. Sometimes this can lead to a merging based on the level of closeness the letter has with the next letter.

o When two letters that have the <u>same genus meet</u> (they have the same exit point but different qualities), <u>the first being saakinah</u> and <u>the second being vowelled</u>, the first will *sometimes* be merged into the second. This is a minor merging of two letters of the same genus (Idghaam Mutajaanisayn Sagheer) *(3.20 complete)*.

o The instances of merging in this case: د <--- ت | ط <--- ت | ت <--- د | ط <--- ت | ت <--- ط

ظ <--- ذ | ذ <--- ث | م <--- ب

o Examples:

يَلْهَث ذَّٰلِكَ   أَثْقَلَت دَّعَوَا   بَسَطَت   إِذ ظَّلَمُوٓا   هَمَّت طَّآئِفَتَانِ   عَبَدتُّمْ

أَرْكَب مَّعَنَا   (This is read as "irkamma'anaa" with an extended nasal sound)

بِسْمِ ٱللَّهِ ٱلرَّحْمَٰنِ ٱلرَّحِيمِ

وَٱلسَّمَآءِ وَٱلطَّارِقِ ﴿١﴾ وَمَآ أَدْرَىٰكَ مَا ٱلطَّارِقُ ﴿٢﴾ ٱلنَّجْمُ ٱلثَّاقِبُ ﴿٣﴾ إِن كُلُّ نَفْسٍ لَّمَّا

عَلَيْهَا حَافِظٌ ﴿٤﴾ فَلْيَنظُرِ ٱلْإِنسَٰنُ مِمَّ خُلِقَ ﴿٥﴾ خُلِقَ مِن مَّآءٍ دَافِقٍ ﴿٦﴾ يَخْرُجُ

مِنۢ بَيْنِ ٱلصُّلْبِ وَٱلتَّرَآئِبِ ﴿٧﴾ إِنَّهُۥ عَلَىٰ رَجْعِهِۦ لَقَادِرٌ ﴿٨﴾ يَوْمَ تُبْلَى ٱلسَّرَآئِرُ ﴿٩﴾

فَمَا لَهُۥ مِن قُوَّةٍ وَلَا نَاصِرٍ ﴿١٠﴾ وَٱلسَّمَآءِ ذَاتِ ٱلرَّجْعِ ﴿١١﴾ وَٱلْأَرْضِ ذَاتِ ٱلصَّدْعِ ﴿١٢﴾

إِنَّهُۥ لَقَوْلٌ فَصْلٌ ﴿١٣﴾ وَمَا هُوَ بِٱلْهَزْلِ ﴿١٤﴾ إِنَّهُمْ يَكِيدُونَ كَيْدًا ﴿١٥﴾ وَأَكِيدُ كَيْدًا

﴿١٦﴾ فَمَهِّلِ ٱلْكَٰفِرِينَ أَمْهِلْهُمْ رُوَيْدًا ﴿١٧﴾

o *Lesson focus-* Focusing on correct pronunciation and application of all rules learnt thus far.

o *Rule-* Letters have different relationships with the letters that follow them. Sometimes this can lead to a merging based on the level of closeness the letter has with the next letter.

o When two letters <u>that are close meet</u> (they have different exit points/qualities but are close to each other), <u>the first being saakinah</u> and <u>the second being vowelled</u>, the first will *sometimes* be merged into the second. This is a minor merging of two letters that are close (Idghaam Mutaqaaribayn Sagheer) *(3.21 complete).*

o The instances of merging in this case:

a) The noon saakinah/tanween merging into و ل م ر ي (the chapter of noon saakinah) e.g.

يُشَاهِدٍ وَ

b) The laam of definiteness (the laam of "Al" found in the beginning of nouns) merging into ت د ذ ر ز س ش ص ض ط ظ ل ن   e.g. ٱلنَّارِ

قُل رَّبِّ

c) The laam saakinah merging into a Raa. An example:

نَخْلُقكُّم

d) The Qaaf saakinah merging into a kaaf. The example: (Al-Mursalat)

بِسۡمِ ٱللَّهِ ٱلرَّحۡمَٰنِ ٱلرَّحِيمِ

وَٱلسَّمَآءِ ذَاتِ ٱلۡبُرُوجِ ﴿١﴾ وَٱلۡيَوۡمِ ٱلۡمَوۡعُودِ ﴿٢﴾ وَشَاهِدٍ وَمَشۡهُودٍ ﴿٣﴾ قُتِلَ أَصۡحَٰبُ ٱلۡأُخۡدُودِ ﴿٤﴾ ٱلنَّارِ ذَاتِ ٱلۡوَقُودِ ﴿٥﴾ إِذۡ هُمۡ عَلَيۡهَا قُعُودٌ ﴿٦﴾ وَهُمۡ عَلَىٰ مَا يَفۡعَلُونَ بِٱلۡمُؤۡمِنِينَ شُهُودٌ ﴿٧﴾ وَمَا نَقَمُوا۟ مِنۡهُمۡ إِلَّآ أَن يُؤۡمِنُوا۟ بِٱللَّهِ ٱلۡعَزِيزِ ٱلۡحَمِيدِ ﴿٨﴾ ٱلَّذِى لَهُۥ مُلۡكُ ٱلسَّمَٰوَٰتِ وَٱلۡأَرۡضِ وَٱللَّهُ عَلَىٰ كُلِّ شَىۡءٍ شَهِيدٌ ﴿٩﴾ إِنَّ ٱلَّذِينَ فَتَنُوا۟ ٱلۡمُؤۡمِنِينَ وَٱلۡمُؤۡمِنَٰتِ ثُمَّ لَمۡ يَتُوبُوا۟ فَلَهُمۡ عَذَابُ جَهَنَّمَ وَلَهُمۡ عَذَابُ ٱلۡحَرِيقِ ﴿١٠﴾

o *Lesson focus*- Focusing on correct pronunciation and application of all rules learnt thus far.

o *Rule*- Letters have different relationships with the letters that follow them. Sometimes this can lead to a merging based on the level of closeness the letter has with the next letter.

o Two distant letters will always be clear and never merge into each other (Idh'haar Mutabaa'idayn) *(3.22 complete).*

إِنَّ ٱلَّذِينَ ءَامَنُوا۟ وَعَمِلُوا۟

ٱلصَّٰلِحَٰتِ لَهُمْ جَنَّٰتٌ تَجْرِى مِن تَحْتِهَا ٱلْأَنْهَٰرُ ذَٰلِكَ ٱلْفَوْزُ ٱلْكَبِيرُ ۝١١

إِنَّ بَطْشَ رَبِّكَ لَشَدِيدٌ ۝١٢ إِنَّهُۥ هُوَ يُبْدِئُ وَيُعِيدُ ۝١٣ وَهُوَ ٱلْغَفُورُ ٱلْوَدُودُ

۝١٤ ذُو ٱلْعَرْشِ ٱلْمَجِيدُ ۝١٥ فَعَّالٌ لِّمَا يُرِيدُ ۝١٦ هَلْ أَتَىٰكَ حَدِيثُ ٱلْجُنُودِ

۝١٧ فِرْعَوْنَ وَثَمُودَ ۝١٨ بَلِ ٱلَّذِينَ كَفَرُوا۟ فِى تَكْذِيبٍ ۝١٩ وَٱللَّهُ مِن وَرَآئِهِم

مُّحِيطٌ ۝٢٠ بَلْ هُوَ قُرْءَانٌ مَّجِيدٌ ۝٢١ فِى لَوْحٍ مَّحْفُوظٍ ۝٢٢

Notes:

....

....

....

....

....

....

o *Lesson focus*- Focusing on correct pronunciation and application of all rules learnt thus far.

o *Rule*- Consolidating all previous rules and taking an opportunity to revise all previous lessons.

بِسْمِ اللَّهِ الرَّحْمَٰنِ الرَّحِيمِ

إِذَا السَّمَاءُ انْشَقَّتْ ﴿١﴾ وَأَذِنَتْ لِرَبِّهَا وَحُقَّتْ ﴿٢﴾ وَإِذَا الْأَرْضُ مُدَّتْ ﴿٣﴾ وَأَلْقَتْ مَا فِيهَا وَتَخَلَّتْ ﴿٤﴾ وَأَذِنَتْ لِرَبِّهَا وَحُقَّتْ ﴿٥﴾ يَا أَيُّهَا الْإِنْسَانُ إِنَّكَ كَادِحٌ إِلَىٰ رَبِّكَ كَدْحًا فَمُلَاقِيهِ ﴿٦﴾ فَأَمَّا مَنْ أُوتِيَ كِتَابَهُ بِيَمِينِهِ ﴿٧﴾ فَسَوْفَ يُحَاسَبُ حِسَابًا يَسِيرًا ﴿٨﴾ وَيَنْقَلِبُ إِلَىٰ أَهْلِهِ مَسْرُورًا ﴿٩﴾ وَأَمَّا مَنْ أُوتِيَ كِتَابَهُ وَرَاءَ ظَهْرِهِ ﴿١٠﴾ فَسَوْفَ يَدْعُو ثُبُورًا ﴿١١﴾ وَيَصْلَىٰ سَعِيرًا ﴿١٢﴾ إِنَّهُ كَانَ فِي أَهْلِهِ مَسْرُورًا ﴿١٣﴾ إِنَّهُ ظَنَّ أَنْ لَنْ يَحُورَ ﴿١٤﴾ بَلَىٰ إِنَّ رَبَّهُ كَانَ بِهِ بَصِيرًا ﴿١٥﴾ فَلَا أُقْسِمُ بِالشَّفَقِ ﴿١٦﴾ وَاللَّيْلِ وَمَا وَسَقَ ﴿١٧﴾ وَالْقَمَرِ إِذَا اتَّسَقَ ﴿١٨﴾ لَتَرْكَبُنَّ طَبَقًا عَنْ طَبَقٍ ﴿١٩﴾ فَمَا لَهُمْ لَا يُؤْمِنُونَ ﴿٢٠﴾ وَإِذَا قُرِئَ عَلَيْهِمُ الْقُرْآنُ لَا يَسْجُدُونَ ۩ ﴿٢١﴾ بَلِ الَّذِينَ كَفَرُوا يُكَذِّبُونَ ﴿٢٢﴾ وَاللَّهُ أَعْلَمُ بِمَا يُوعُونَ ﴿٢٣﴾ فَبَشِّرْهُمْ بِعَذَابٍ أَلِيمٍ ﴿٢٤﴾ إِلَّا الَّذِينَ آمَنُوا وَعَمِلُوا الصَّالِحَاتِ لَهُمْ أَجْرٌ غَيْرُ مَمْنُونٍ ﴿٢٥﴾

Notes:

....

....

....

....

o *Lesson focus-* Focusing on correct pronunciation and application of all rules learnt thus far.

o *Rule-* Sometimes, the merging is considered **_complete_**. This means that the first letter completely merges into the second and no trace of it is left (Idghaam Kaamil) *(3.23 complete)*.

o We know that the merging will be complete if both letters are of the same strength or the first letter is weaker than the second.

أَو وَزَنُوهُمْ   قُلُوبِهِم مَّا كَانُوا   وَيْلٌ لِّلْمُطَفِّفِينَ

o *Examples:*

بِسْمِ اللَّهِ الرَّحْمَٰنِ الرَّحِيمِ

وَيْلٌ لِّلْمُطَفِّفِينَ ﴿١﴾ ٱلَّذِينَ إِذَا ٱكْتَالُوا عَلَى ٱلنَّاسِ يَسْتَوْفُونَ ﴿٢﴾ وَإِذَا كَالُوهُمْ أَو وَّزَنُوهُمْ يُخْسِرُونَ ﴿٣﴾ أَلَا يَظُنُّ أُولَٰئِكَ أَنَّهُم مَّبْعُوثُونَ ﴿٤﴾ لِيَوْمٍ عَظِيمٍ ﴿٥﴾ يَوْمَ يَقُومُ ٱلنَّاسُ لِرَبِّ ٱلْعَٰلَمِينَ ﴿٦﴾ كَلَّا إِنَّ كِتَٰبَ ٱلْفُجَّارِ لَفِي سِجِّينٍ ﴿٧﴾ وَمَا أَدْرَاكَ مَا سِجِّينٌ ﴿٨﴾ كِتَٰبٌ مَّرْقُومٌ ﴿٩﴾ وَيْلٌ يَوْمَئِذٍ لِّلْمُكَذِّبِينَ ﴿١٠﴾ ٱلَّذِينَ يُكَذِّبُونَ بِيَوْمِ ٱلدِّينِ ﴿١١﴾ وَمَا يُكَذِّبُ بِهِ إِلَّا كُلُّ مُعْتَدٍ أَثِيمٍ ﴿١٢﴾ إِذَا تُتْلَىٰ عَلَيْهِ ءَايَٰتُنَا قَالَ أَسَٰطِيرُ ٱلْأَوَّلِينَ ﴿١٣﴾ كَلَّا بَلْ رَانَ عَلَىٰ قُلُوبِهِم مَّا كَانُوا يَكْسِبُونَ ﴿١٤﴾ كَلَّا إِنَّهُمْ عَن رَّبِّهِمْ يَوْمَئِذٍ لَّمَحْجُوبُونَ ﴿١٥﴾ ثُمَّ إِنَّهُمْ لَصَالُوا ٱلْجَحِيمِ ﴿١٦﴾ ثُمَّ يُقَالُ هَٰذَا ٱلَّذِي كُنتُم بِهِ تُكَذِّبُونَ ﴿١٧﴾

Notes:

....

....

....

....

o *Lesson focus-* Focusing on correct pronunciation and application of all rules learnt thus far.

o *Rule-* Sometimes, the merging is considered <u>*incomplete*</u>. This means that the first letter incompletely merges into the second and there is still a trace of the first letter that remains. This trace could be, for example, the nasal sound for the noon or meem or the heaviness of the TAA that merges into a taa (Idghaam Naaqis) *(3.24 complete)*.

o We know that the merging will be incomplete if the first letter is stronger than the second.

o *Examples:* بَسَطَتْ مِسْكٌ وَ عَيْنًا يَشْرَبُ

o *Tip:* When the merging is complete there will be a shaddah on the second letter, if it is incomplete there is no shaddah on the second letter.

كَلَّا إِنَّ

كِتَبَ ٱلْأَبْرَارِ لَفِى عِلِّيِّينَ ۝ وَمَآ أَدْرَىٰكَ مَا عِلِّيُّونَ ۝ كِتَبٌ مَّرْقُومٌ ۝ يَشْهَدُهُ ٱلْمُقَرَّبُونَ ۝ إِنَّ ٱلْأَبْرَارَ لَفِى نَعِيمٍ ۝ عَلَى ٱلْأَرَآئِكِ يَنظُرُونَ ۝ تَعْرِفُ فِى وُجُوهِهِمْ نَضْرَةَ ٱلنَّعِيمِ ۝ يُسْقَوْنَ مِن رَّحِيقٍ مَّخْتُومٍ ۝ خِتَمُهُ مِسْكٌ وَفِى ذَٰلِكَ فَلْيَتَنَافَسِ ٱلْمُتَنَافِسُونَ ۝ وَمِزَاجُهُ مِن تَسْنِيمٍ ۝ عَيْنًا يَشْرَبُ بِهَا ٱلْمُقَرَّبُونَ ۝ إِنَّ ٱلَّذِينَ أَجْرَمُوا۟ كَانُوا۟ مِنَ ٱلَّذِينَ ءَامَنُوا۟ يَضْحَكُونَ ۝ وَإِذَا مَرُّوا۟ بِهِمْ يَتَغَامَزُونَ ۝ وَإِذَا ٱنقَلَبُوٓا۟ إِلَىٰٓ أَهْلِهِمُ ٱنقَلَبُوا۟ فَكِهِينَ ۝ وَإِذَا رَأَوْهُمْ قَالُوٓا۟ إِنَّ هَٰٓؤُلَآءِ لَضَآلُّونَ ۝ وَمَآ أُرْسِلُوا۟ عَلَيْهِمْ حَفِظِينَ ۝ فَٱلْيَوْمَ ٱلَّذِينَ ءَامَنُوا۟ مِنَ ٱلْكُفَّارِ يَضْحَكُونَ ۝ عَلَى ٱلْأَرَآئِكِ يَنظُرُونَ ۝ هَلْ ثُوِّبَ ٱلْكُفَّارُ مَا كَانُوا۟ يَفْعَلُونَ ۝

o *Lesson focus*- Focusing on correct pronunciation and application of all rules learnt thus far.

o *Rule*- Alongside the preliminaries and exit points, all rules of Tajweed have been covered throughout the course of the previous lessons. Al hamdu liLlah. Focus completely on annotation, correct pronunciation and application of all rules.

بِسۡمِ ٱللَّهِ ٱلرَّحۡمَٰنِ ٱلرَّحِيمِ

إِذَا ٱلسَّمَآءُ ٱنفَطَرَتۡ ﴿١﴾ وَإِذَا ٱلۡكَوَاكِبُ ٱنتَثَرَتۡ ﴿٢﴾ وَإِذَا ٱلۡبِحَارُ فُجِّرَتۡ ﴿٣﴾ وَإِذَا ٱلۡقُبُورُ بُعۡثِرَتۡ ﴿٤﴾ عَلِمَتۡ نَفۡسٌ مَّا قَدَّمَتۡ وَأَخَّرَتۡ ﴿٥﴾ يَٰٓأَيُّهَا ٱلۡإِنسَٰنُ مَا غَرَّكَ بِرَبِّكَ ٱلۡكَرِيمِ ﴿٦﴾ ٱلَّذِي خَلَقَكَ فَسَوَّىٰكَ فَعَدَلَكَ ﴿٧﴾ فِىٓ أَيِّ صُورَةٍ مَّا شَآءَ رَكَّبَكَ ﴿٨﴾ كَلَّا بَلۡ تُكَذِّبُونَ بِٱلدِّينِ ﴿٩﴾ وَإِنَّ عَلَيۡكُمۡ لَحَٰفِظِينَ ﴿١٠﴾ كِرَامًا كَٰتِبِينَ ﴿١١﴾ يَعۡلَمُونَ مَا تَفۡعَلُونَ ﴿١٢﴾ إِنَّ ٱلۡأَبۡرَارَ لَفِى نَعِيمٍ ﴿١٣﴾ وَإِنَّ ٱلۡفُجَّارَ لَفِى جَحِيمٍ ﴿١٤﴾ يَصۡلَوۡنَهَا يَوۡمَ ٱلدِّينِ ﴿١٥﴾ وَمَا هُمۡ عَنۡهَا بِغَآئِبِينَ ﴿١٦﴾ وَمَآ أَدۡرَىٰكَ مَا يَوۡمُ ٱلدِّينِ ﴿١٧﴾ ثُمَّ مَآ أَدۡرَىٰكَ مَا يَوۡمُ ٱلدِّينِ ﴿١٨﴾ يَوۡمَ لَا تَمۡلِكُ نَفۡسٌ لِّنَفۡسٍ شَيۡئًا وَٱلۡأَمۡرُ يَوۡمَئِذٍ لِّلَّهِ ﴿١٩﴾

Notes:

....

....

....

....

o *Lesson focus*- Focusing on correct pronunciation and application of all rules learnt thus far.

بِسْمِ اللَّهِ الرَّحْمَٰنِ الرَّحِيمِ

إِذَا الشَّمْسُ كُوِّرَتْ ﴿١﴾ وَإِذَا النُّجُومُ انكَدَرَتْ ﴿٢﴾ وَإِذَا الْجِبَالُ سُيِّرَتْ ﴿٣﴾ وَإِذَا الْعِشَارُ عُطِّلَتْ ﴿٤﴾ وَإِذَا الْوُحُوشُ حُشِرَتْ ﴿٥﴾ وَإِذَا الْبِحَارُ سُجِّرَتْ ﴿٦﴾ وَإِذَا النُّفُوسُ زُوِّجَتْ ﴿٧﴾ وَإِذَا الْمَوْءُودَةُ سُئِلَتْ ﴿٨﴾ بِأَيِّ ذَنبٍ قُتِلَتْ ﴿٩﴾ وَإِذَا الصُّحُفُ نُشِرَتْ ﴿١٠﴾ وَإِذَا السَّمَاءُ كُشِطَتْ ﴿١١﴾ وَإِذَا الْجَحِيمُ سُعِّرَتْ ﴿١٢﴾ وَإِذَا الْجَنَّةُ أُزْلِفَتْ ﴿١٣﴾ عَلِمَتْ نَفْسٌ مَّا أَحْضَرَتْ ﴿١٤﴾ فَلَا أُقْسِمُ بِالْخُنَّسِ ﴿١٥﴾ الْجَوَارِ الْكُنَّسِ ﴿١٦﴾ وَاللَّيْلِ إِذَا عَسْعَسَ ﴿١٧﴾ وَالصُّبْحِ إِذَا تَنَفَّسَ ﴿١٨﴾ إِنَّهُ لَقَوْلُ رَسُولٍ كَرِيمٍ ﴿١٩﴾ ذِي قُوَّةٍ عِندَ ذِي الْعَرْشِ مَكِينٍ ﴿٢٠﴾ مُّطَاعٍ ثَمَّ أَمِينٍ ﴿٢١﴾ وَمَا صَاحِبُكُم بِمَجْنُونٍ ﴿٢٢﴾ وَلَقَدْ رَآهُ بِالْأُفُقِ الْمُبِينِ ﴿٢٣﴾ وَمَا هُوَ عَلَى الْغَيْبِ بِضَنِينٍ ﴿٢٤﴾ وَمَا هُوَ بِقَوْلِ شَيْطَانٍ رَّجِيمٍ ﴿٢٥﴾ فَأَيْنَ تَذْهَبُونَ ﴿٢٦﴾ إِنْ هُوَ إِلَّا ذِكْرٌ لِّلْعَالَمِينَ ﴿٢٧﴾ لِمَن شَاءَ مِنكُمْ أَن يَسْتَقِيمَ ﴿٢٨﴾ وَمَا تَشَاءُونَ إِلَّا أَن يَشَاءَ اللَّهُ رَبُّ الْعَالَمِينَ ﴿٢٩﴾

Notes:

....

....

....

....

o *Lesson focus*- Focusing on correct pronunciation and application of all rules learnt thus far.

بِسْمِ اللَّهِ الرَّحْمَنِ الرَّحِيمِ

عَبَسَ وَتَوَلَّىٰ ﴿١﴾ أَن جَاءَهُ الْأَعْمَىٰ ﴿٢﴾ وَمَا يُدْرِيكَ لَعَلَّهُ يَزَّكَّىٰ ﴿٣﴾ أَوْ يَذَّكَّرُ ﴿٤﴾ فَتَنفَعَهُ الذِّكْرَىٰ ﴿٤﴾ أَمَّا مَنِ اسْتَغْنَىٰ ﴿٥﴾ فَأَنتَ لَهُ تَصَدَّىٰ ﴿٦﴾ وَمَا عَلَيْكَ أَلَّا يَزَّكَّىٰ ﴿٧﴾ وَأَمَّا مَن جَاءَكَ يَسْعَىٰ ﴿٨﴾ وَهُوَ يَخْشَىٰ ﴿٩﴾ فَأَنتَ عَنْهُ تَلَهَّىٰ ﴿١٠﴾ كَلَّا إِنَّهَا تَذْكِرَةٌ ﴿١١﴾ فَمَن شَاءَ ذَكَرَهُ ﴿١٢﴾ فِي صُحُفٍ مُّكَرَّمَةٍ ﴿١٣﴾ مَّرْفُوعَةٍ مُّطَهَّرَةٍ ﴿١٤﴾ بِأَيْدِي سَفَرَةٍ ﴿١٥﴾ كِرَامٍ بَرَرَةٍ ﴿١٦﴾ قُتِلَ الْإِنسَانُ مَا أَكْفَرَهُ ﴿١٧﴾ مِنْ أَيِّ شَيْءٍ خَلَقَهُ ﴿١٨﴾ مِن نُّطْفَةٍ خَلَقَهُ فَقَدَّرَهُ ﴿١٩﴾ ثُمَّ السَّبِيلَ يَسَّرَهُ ﴿٢٠﴾ ثُمَّ أَمَاتَهُ فَأَقْبَرَهُ ﴿٢١﴾ ثُمَّ إِذَا شَاءَ أَنشَرَهُ ﴿٢٢﴾

Notes:

....

....

....

....

....

....

....

....

....

o *Lesson focus*- Focusing on correct pronunciation and application of all rules learnt thus far.

كَلَّا لَمَّا يَقْضِ مَا أَمَرَهُ ﴿٢٣﴾ فَلْيَنظُرِ
ٱلْإِنسَٰنُ إِلَىٰ طَعَامِهِ ﴿٢٤﴾ أَنَّا صَبَبْنَا ٱلْمَآءَ صَبًّا ﴿٢٥﴾ ثُمَّ شَقَقْنَا ٱلْأَرْضَ شَقًّا ﴿٢٦﴾
فَأَنۢبَتْنَا فِيهَا حَبًّا ﴿٢٧﴾ وَعِنَبًا وَقَضْبًا ﴿٢٨﴾ وَزَيْتُونًا وَنَخْلًا ﴿٢٩﴾ وَحَدَآئِقَ غُلْبًا ﴿٣٠﴾
وَفَٰكِهَةً وَأَبًّا ﴿٣١﴾ مَّتَٰعًا لَّكُمْ وَلِأَنْعَٰمِكُمْ ﴿٣٢﴾ فَإِذَا جَآءَتِ ٱلصَّآخَّةُ ﴿٣٣﴾ يَوْمَ
يَفِرُّ ٱلْمَرْءُ مِنْ أَخِيهِ ﴿٣٤﴾ وَأُمِّهِ وَأَبِيهِ ﴿٣٥﴾ وَصَٰحِبَتِهِ وَبَنِيهِ ﴿٣٦﴾ لِكُلِّ ٱمْرِئٍ
مِّنْهُمْ يَوْمَئِذٍ شَأْنٌ يُغْنِيهِ ﴿٣٧﴾ وُجُوهٌ يَوْمَئِذٍ مُّسْفِرَةٌ ﴿٣٨﴾ ضَاحِكَةٌ مُّسْتَبْشِرَةٌ
﴿٣٩﴾ وَوُجُوهٌ يَوْمَئِذٍ عَلَيْهَا غَبَرَةٌ ﴿٤٠﴾ تَرْهَقُهَا قَتَرَةٌ ﴿٤١﴾ أُوْلَٰٓئِكَ هُمُ ٱلْكَفَرَةُ ٱلْفَجَرَةُ
﴿٤٢﴾

Notes:

....

....

....

....

....

....

....

....

....

o *Lesson focus-* Focusing on correct pronunciation and application of all rules learnt thus far.

بِسْمِ اللَّهِ الرَّحْمَٰنِ الرَّحِيمِ

وَالنَّازِعَاتِ غَرْقًا ﴿١﴾ وَالنَّاشِطَاتِ نَشْطًا ﴿٢﴾ وَالسَّابِحَاتِ سَبْحًا ﴿٣﴾

فَالسَّابِقَاتِ سَبْقًا ﴿٤﴾ فَالْمُدَبِّرَاتِ أَمْرًا ﴿٥﴾ يَوْمَ تَرْجُفُ الرَّاجِفَةُ ﴿٦﴾ تَتْبَعُهَا

الرَّادِفَةُ ﴿٧﴾ قُلُوبٌ يَوْمَئِذٍ وَاجِفَةٌ ﴿٨﴾ أَبْصَارُهَا خَاشِعَةٌ ﴿٩﴾ يَقُولُونَ

أَإِنَّا لَمَرْدُودُونَ فِي الْحَافِرَةِ ﴿١٠﴾ أَإِذَا كُنَّا عِظَامًا نَّخِرَةً ﴿١١﴾ قَالُوا تِلْكَ

إِذًا كَرَّةٌ خَاسِرَةٌ ﴿١٢﴾ فَإِنَّمَا هِيَ زَجْرَةٌ وَاحِدَةٌ ﴿١٣﴾ فَإِذَا هُم بِالسَّاهِرَةِ ﴿١٤﴾

هَلْ أَتَاكَ حَدِيثُ مُوسَىٰ ﴿١٥﴾ إِذْ نَادَاهُ رَبُّهُ بِالْوَادِ الْمُقَدَّسِ طُوًى ﴿١٦﴾ اذْهَبْ

إِلَىٰ فِرْعَوْنَ إِنَّهُ طَغَىٰ ﴿١٧﴾ فَقُلْ هَل لَّكَ إِلَىٰ أَن تَزَكَّىٰ ﴿١٨﴾ وَأَهْدِيَكَ إِلَىٰ رَبِّكَ

فَتَخْشَىٰ ﴿١٩﴾ فَأَرَاهُ الْآيَةَ الْكُبْرَىٰ ﴿٢٠﴾ فَكَذَّبَ وَعَصَىٰ ﴿٢١﴾ ثُمَّ أَدْبَرَ يَسْعَىٰ

﴿٢٢﴾ فَحَشَرَ فَنَادَىٰ ﴿٢٣﴾ فَقَالَ أَنَا رَبُّكُمُ الْأَعْلَىٰ ﴿٢٤﴾ فَأَخَذَهُ اللَّهُ نَكَالَ الْآخِرَةِ

وَالْأُولَىٰ ﴿٢٥﴾ إِنَّ فِي ذَٰلِكَ لَعِبْرَةً لِّمَن يَخْشَىٰ ﴿٢٦﴾

Notes:

....

....

o *Lesson focus*- Focusing on correct pronunciation and application of all rules learnt thus far.

ءَأَنتُمْ أَشَدُّ خَلْقًا أَمِ ٱلسَّمَآءُ بَنَىٰهَا

﴿٢٧﴾ رَفَعَ سَمْكَهَا فَسَوَّىٰهَا ﴿٢٨﴾ وَأَغْطَشَ لَيْلَهَا وَأَخْرَجَ ضُحَىٰهَا ﴿٢٩﴾ وَٱلْأَرْضَ

بَعْدَ ذَٰلِكَ دَحَىٰهَآ ﴿٣٠﴾ أَخْرَجَ مِنْهَا مَآءَهَا وَمَرْعَىٰهَا ﴿٣١﴾ وَٱلْجِبَالَ أَرْسَىٰهَا

﴿٣٢﴾ مَتَٰعًا لَّكُمْ وَلِأَنْعَٰمِكُمْ ﴿٣٣﴾ فَإِذَا جَآءَتِ ٱلطَّآمَّةُ ٱلْكُبْرَىٰ ﴿٣٤﴾ يَوْمَ

يَتَذَكَّرُ ٱلْإِنسَٰنُ مَا سَعَىٰ ﴿٣٥﴾ وَبُرِّزَتِ ٱلْجَحِيمُ لِمَن يَرَىٰ ﴿٣٦﴾ فَأَمَّا مَن طَغَىٰ

﴿٣٧﴾ وَءَاثَرَ ٱلْحَيَوٰةَ ٱلدُّنْيَا ﴿٣٨﴾ فَإِنَّ ٱلْجَحِيمَ هِيَ ٱلْمَأْوَىٰ ﴿٣٩﴾ وَأَمَّا مَنْ خَافَ

مَقَامَ رَبِّهِۦ وَنَهَى ٱلنَّفْسَ عَنِ ٱلْهَوَىٰ ﴿٤٠﴾ فَإِنَّ ٱلْجَنَّةَ هِيَ ٱلْمَأْوَىٰ ﴿٤١﴾

يَسْـَٔلُونَكَ عَنِ ٱلسَّاعَةِ أَيَّانَ مُرْسَىٰهَا ﴿٤٢﴾ فِيمَ أَنتَ مِن ذِكْرَىٰهَآ ﴿٤٣﴾ إِلَىٰ رَبِّكَ

مُنتَهَىٰهَآ ﴿٤٤﴾ إِنَّمَآ أَنتَ مُنذِرُ مَن يَخْشَىٰهَا ﴿٤٥﴾ كَأَنَّهُمْ يَوْمَ يَرَوْنَهَا لَمْ يَلْبَثُوٓا۟

إِلَّا عَشِيَّةً أَوْ ضُحَىٰهَا ﴿٤٦﴾

Notes:

....

....

....

....

....

....

o *Lesson focus*- Focusing on correct pronunciation and application of all rules learnt thus far.

بِسْمِ اللَّهِ الرَّحْمَنِ الرَّحِيمِ

عَمَّ يَتَسَاءَلُونَ ﴿١﴾ عَنِ النَّبَإِ الْعَظِيمِ ﴿٢﴾ الَّذِى هُمْ فِيهِ مُخْتَلِفُونَ ﴿٣﴾ كَلَّا سَيَعْلَمُونَ ﴿٤﴾ ثُمَّ كَلَّا سَيَعْلَمُونَ ﴿٥﴾ أَلَمْ نَجْعَلِ الْأَرْضَ مِهَادًا ﴿٦﴾ وَالْجِبَالَ أَوْتَادًا ﴿٧﴾ وَخَلَقْنَاكُمْ أَزْوَاجًا ﴿٨﴾ وَجَعَلْنَا نَوْمَكُمْ سُبَاتًا ﴿٩﴾ وَجَعَلْنَا اللَّيْلَ لِبَاسًا ﴿١٠﴾ وَجَعَلْنَا النَّهَارَ مَعَاشًا ﴿١١﴾ وَبَنَيْنَا فَوْقَكُمْ سَبْعًا شِدَادًا ﴿١٢﴾ وَجَعَلْنَا سِرَاجًا وَهَّاجًا ﴿١٣﴾ وَأَنْزَلْنَا مِنَ الْمُعْصِرَاتِ مَاءً ثَجَّاجًا ﴿١٤﴾ لِنُخْرِجَ بِهِ حَبًّا وَنَبَاتًا ﴿١٥﴾ وَجَنَّاتٍ أَلْفَافًا ﴿١٦﴾ إِنَّ يَوْمَ الْفَصْلِ كَانَ مِيقَاتًا ﴿١٧﴾ يَوْمَ يُنْفَخُ فِي الصُّورِ فَتَأْتُونَ أَفْوَاجًا ﴿١٨﴾ وَفُتِحَتِ السَّمَاءُ فَكَانَتْ أَبْوَابًا ﴿١٩﴾ وَسُيِّرَتِ الْجِبَالُ فَكَانَتْ سَرَابًا ﴿٢٠﴾

Notes:

....
....
....
....
....
....
....
....

o *Lesson focus*- Focusing on correct pronunciation and application of all rules learnt thus far.

إِنَّ جَهَنَّمَ كَانَتْ مِرْصَادًا

لِّلطَّاغِينَ مَآبًا ﴿٢٢﴾ لَّٰبِثِينَ فِيهَآ أَحْقَابًا ﴿٢٣﴾ لَّا يَذُوقُونَ فِيهَا بَرْدًا ﴿٢١﴾

وَلَا شَرَابًا ﴿٢٤﴾ إِلَّا حَمِيمًا وَغَسَّاقًا ﴿٢٥﴾ جَزَآءً وِفَاقًا ﴿٢٦﴾ إِنَّهُمْ كَانُوا

لَا يَرْجُونَ حِسَابًا ﴿٢٧﴾ وَكَذَّبُوا بِآيَاتِنَا كِذَّابًا ﴿٢٨﴾ وَكُلَّ شَيْءٍ

أَحْصَيْنَاهُ كِتَابًا ﴿٢٩﴾ فَذُوقُوا فَلَن نَّزِيدَكُمْ إِلَّا عَذَابًا ﴿٣٠﴾ إِنَّ

لِلْمُتَّقِينَ مَفَازًا ﴿٣١﴾ حَدَآئِقَ وَأَعْنَابًا ﴿٣٢﴾ وَكَوَاعِبَ أَتْرَابًا ﴿٣٣﴾ وَكَأْسًا دِهَاقًا ﴿٣٤﴾

لَّا يَسْمَعُونَ فِيهَا لَغْوًا وَلَا كِذَّابًا ﴿٣٥﴾ جَزَآءً مِّن رَّبِّكَ عَطَآءً حِسَابًا ﴿٣٦﴾ رَّبِّ

السَّمَاوَاتِ وَالْأَرْضِ وَمَا بَيْنَهُمَا الرَّحْمَٰنِ لَا يَمْلِكُونَ مِنْهُ خِطَابًا ﴿٣٧﴾ يَوْمَ يَقُومُ

الرُّوحُ وَالْمَلَائِكَةُ صَفًّا لَّا يَتَكَلَّمُونَ إِلَّا مَنْ أَذِنَ لَهُ الرَّحْمَٰنُ وَقَالَ صَوَابًا

﴿٣٨﴾ ذَٰلِكَ الْيَوْمُ الْحَقُّ فَمَن شَآءَ اتَّخَذَ إِلَىٰ رَبِّهِ مَآبًا ﴿٣٩﴾ إِنَّآ

أَنذَرْنَاكُمْ عَذَابًا قَرِيبًا يَوْمَ يَنظُرُ الْمَرْءُ مَا قَدَّمَتْ يَدَاهُ وَيَقُولُ الْكَافِرُ

يَٰلَيْتَنِي كُنتُ تُرَابًا ﴿٤٠﴾

Notes:

....

....

....

Conclusion

By the immense grace of Allah Ta'alaa, we have come to the conclusion of Juz 'Amma. It is hoped that the learning and application of the main Tajweed rules have been facilitated throughout this small work. It has been my earnest desire to allow beginning students of the Qur'an to access the Qur'an in a natural, easy manner. At the same time, it is important to transmit the knowledge imparted unto us with precision and accuracy. As such, sometimes the fine points may have been difficult to digest- for this I apologise.

The journey of the student of the Qur'an does not end at this stage. For the one who strives to be a devoted slave of Allah the best pathway he can traverse is the path of the Qur'an. The Qur'an is a book of divine guidance and benevolence, its seeker can be certain to find closeness to his Lord at the end of the road, inshaa Allah. However, this requires a sincere struggle and truthfulness with Allah Ta'alaa.

From this point on, I would advise the student to continue reciting to their teacher and commence learning the various texts on Tajweed, inshaa Allah. The door of Qur'anic memorisation should also have opened by this point- a student may gently and gradually start this journey with determination, inshaa Allah.

Lastly, I ask that anyone who benefits from this work makes supplication for the compiler and that any mistakes are pardoned. Those of expertise are free to discuss and raise concerns. May Allah Ta'alaa accept it from us and forgive us. Ameen.

Bint 'Abd Al Hannan Al Britaaniyyah

sisterskhidmah@gmail.com

13 Ramadhan, 1444AH

04/04/2023

Notes:

....
....
....
....
....
....
....
....
....
....
....
....
....
....
....
....
....
....
....
....
....
....
....
....
....

Printed in Great Britain
by Amazon

22752256R00044